FINDING COMMON GROUND

FINDING COMMON GROUND

HOW TO

COMMUNICATE

WITH THOSE

OUTSIDE THE

CHRISTIAN

COMMUNITY...

WHILE WE

STILL CAN

TIM DOWNS

MOODY PRESS
CHICAGO

ISBN: 0-8024-4096-7

1 3 5 7 9 10 8 6 4 2

Printed in the United States of America

For the staff of the Communication Center
past and present, fellow tillers of the soil

And for my beautiful Joy,
who helps God hold all things
together in my life

CONTENTS

ACKNOWLEDGMENTS

Thanks to my talented editor, Cheryl Dunlop, for lending both her editorial and diplomatic skills to this project.

Thanks to my good friend and sounding board, Kent Kramer, for helping me over the years to shape the thoughts that became this book.

Thanks to my colleague Tim Muehlhoff, who advised me to edit out thousands of words without offering even one to take their place. It's a better book because of you.

Thanks to my beautiful wife, Joy, the true writer of our family, who postponed her career to sow to the next generation. Thanks for your love, advice, and encouragement.

Thanks to my three wonderful kids, Tommy, Erin, and Kelsey, the next generation of believers by God's grace. This book was written for your benefit.

And a special thanks to the staff of Campus Crusade for Christ, who spend each day cultivating, planting, nurturing, and harvesting all over the world.

INTRODUCTION

In this book I will say a dozen things that are perfectly obvious; I will make seven statements that are completely faithful but not as conspicuous; I will argue five doubtful things that I nonetheless believe to be true; and I will suggest two ideas that will sound like heresy.

Let the reader note: These ideas will sound like heresy, but they violate no biblical principle or precept. They may violate what I like to call "private" doctrines: personal convictions that are so firmly believed that we unconsciously ascribe to them near-biblical authority. I believe it's a healthy thing from time to time to attempt to distinguish our private doctrines from those truly found in Scripture, to keep the Bible from constantly increasing in size.

First, I will suggest that, though a great number of evangelicals are absolutely certain that Christ will return in this generation, He might not. I am not saying that He will not; I am saying that I don't know. To put it even more boldly, I am suggesting that no one else knows either. This issue certainly comprises a private doctrine for many Christians, and readers who possess far more certainty about this issue may think me lacking in faith or ignorant of the signs of the times. They may feel confident, as one scholar put it, that "God will not be able to bear this wicked world much longer, but will come, with the dreadful day, and chastise the scorners of his Word."

That was written by Martin Luther, four centuries ago.

Will Christ return in our generation? The biblical response seems to be this: Live as though He will, and plan as though He won't. I am to live each day with a readiness and anticipation of His coming, but I am still to live responsibly with a view to the future—even the distant future. Luther was once asked, "If you knew for certain that Christ will return tomorrow, what would you do today?" He replied, "I would plant a tree." In this book I will recommend that American Christians plant a few trees—a whole lot of them, in fact. The forestry project that I'm recommending requires a far-sightedness that is currently unpopular in the Christian community. In the last days, I have written a book about the future.

Second, I will suggest that sometimes not telling someone everything you know about Jesus and the Bible is an act of faith, love, and courage. In this book I will introduce the concepts of "harvesting" and "sowing." By harvesting, I mean what we traditionally refer to as evangelism: the attempt to communicate the complete gospel message to a listener and to lead that person to Christ. By sowing, I mean the slow, gradual, behind-the-scenes work that prepares a listener—or an entire culture—to be able to hear the gospel. Many evangelicals, convinced that these are the last days, believe that we are living in the time of the Last, Great Harvest. In our enthusiasm for the harvest we have forgotten the role of the sower—but as Luther said, it is always a time to sow. This book has two purposes: to remind Christians of the critical need to sow in our nation, and to warn of the tragic consequences if we do not.

This book is about the crucial job of *finding common ground* between the Christian and secular worlds, two vast continents that are rapidly drifting apart. It's a book about the forgotten art of the sower. And it's a reminder to this generation of Christians that we have a responsibility to help prepare for the harvest of the next.

Chapter 1 | THE PARABLE OF THE SOIL

Once upon a time there was a farmer who lived with his family on a great farm. Each spring he went out to his fields to sow. As he wandered through his fields, scattering grain to and fro, he watched the tiny seeds disappear into the cracks in the earth. *How I hate to sow,* he thought to himself. *I shall have to wait weeks before the seedlings even appear.*

All summer the farmer tended his fields. He hoed the long furrows to loosen the soil around the young plants, he watered the thirsty roots, and he pulled away the choking weeds. *How I hate to tend the fields,* he thought. *I shall have to bend my back and wipe my brow for three more months before the harvest.*

Finally the harvest season came. The farmer waded through the thick, golden bounty. He bundled great sheaves of grain, he gathered great clusters of grapes from dewy vines, and he plucked scarlet fruit from the bowing trees. *How I love to harvest,* he thought. *I will hold a great feast. My wife will bake the bread and my children will press the grapes. We will eat and drink and rest from our labor.*

When the feast was over, the farmer began to think about the planting season ahead. *The harvest is scarcely over,* he brooded, *and already I must turn under my fields and prepare for the next season. How I hate to sow. How I hate to tend the fields. But I love to harvest!* So the farmer decided then and there that he would no longer sow or water or weed. He would only harvest.

The farmer returned to his fields. There he found grain the gatherers had missed and fruit the pickers had not been able to reach. So the farmer continued to harvest. "From now on," said the farmer, "every day will be a harvest, and every night will be a feast."

But the harvest was thin. Each day, as the land grew more and more desolate, the farmer continued to wander through his fields. He plucked an occasional piece of shriveled fruit or picked up a fallen ear of grain. He continued to do what he loved to do until there was nothing left to gather at all. But still, each day he walked through his fields, swinging his scythe over arid ground or tugging at the brittle twigs of a barren tree.

In the spring, when it was time for the new seedlings to emerge, the farmer's fields were still bare. Seed that had fallen during the harvest could not break through the crusty soil that had felt no plow. The few tender plants that emerged soon parched and withered without water. Only thick, thorny weeds could survive. They scratched the farmer's arms and tore at his clothing as he drifted through his fields, still looking for something to harvest.

At last the farmer's children cried out, "Alas, Father, what have you done to us? You have harvested but you have not sown, and now the fields are hard and lifeless. You have gathered the last harvest, and now your children will starve. There is nothing left for us but to move to a new land where the fields are still fertile."

So the farmer and his family loaded their wagon and rolled away.

Harvesting for Christ in the New Millennium

This is not a book about farming. This is a book about the time in which we live: the end of the twentieth century and beginning of the twenty-first. The end of the second millennium. Some say the end of time.

It's about the year 2000, and what many Christians believe is our one final chance to fulfill the Great Commission.

It's about the Last, Great Harvest. It's about the evangelical world's commitment to break up the fallow ground, send every worker into the harvest, and make one last-ditch effort to reach our country and the world for Jesus Christ. It's about the aspect of the harvest many workers have forgotten: the need to sow, even as we harvest, and to prepare for a harvest still to come.

The fourth chapter of the gospel of John contains the well-known encounter between Jesus and the woman at the well. The woman hurried into the city of Sychar to tell everyone about "a man who told me all the things that I have done" (v. 29). As curious men poured from the city to investigate this phenomenon firsthand, Jesus turned His attention to His disciples. "Do you not say, 'Four months more and then the harvest'?" (v. 35 NIV). Jesus was quoting a familiar proverb of the day, the equivalent of our "All things come to him who waits." But there would be no waiting here. For generations past, God had sown the Semitic soil with the words of His prophets and watered it with the blood of His faithful messengers and servants. Now, in the fullness of time, He had sent forth His Son. This was no time to stand idly by. This was a season of harvest.

"I tell you, open your eyes and look at the fields!" Jesus urged them. "They are ripe for harvest. Even now the reaper draws his wages, even now he harvests the crop for eternal life . . ." (vv. 35b–36 NIV).

Harvesting What Others Have Sown

The Master Farmer was about to turn the work of harvesting over to His laborers—ignorant, ungrateful laborers. The disciples were like farmhands not hired until the beginning of the harvest season. They had missed the backbreaking labor of the spring plowing and seeding. They had no callused ridges from harrow or hoe. Their backs were not bent from pruning; their necks were not thick and leathery from the summer sun. They were hired in the cool of the autumn, when the fruit hung low on the trees and the heads of grain could be picked without stooping. They could *enjoy* the harvest, but they could never fully *appreciate* it until they understood the contribution of those who had come before them. Worst of all, they were in danger of spiritual pride. From a human perspective, who should really take credit for this harvest? The rooster crows, but it's the hen that laid the egg.

So the Farmer spoke to the farmhands: "Even now the reaper draws his wages, even now he harvests the crop for eternal life, so that the sower and the reaper may be glad together. Thus the saying 'One sows and another reaps' is true. I sent you to reap what you have not worked for. Others have done the hard work, and you have reaped the benefits of their labor" (John 4:36–38 NIV).

Welcome to the harvest, Jesus said. *Have a good time, but don't get cocky. Remember, this is not your harvest—it's Mine. Some planted, others watered, but I made it grow. So neither he who plants nor he who waters is anything, but only God, who makes things grow. You're just fellow workers, hired harvesters—and you're not even harvesting your own crop. You know the old saying, "One sows and another reaps." You know what it feels like to be the sower and to see someone else reap the benefit of all your labors. Remember what Solomon said? "I hated all the fruit of my labor for which I had labored under the sun, for I must leave it to the man who will come after me." This time you're the reapers, and you're about to reap what generations before you tirelessly and thanklessly sowed. Without them, there would be no harvest. Don't forget it.*

Both the farmer and the Christian love to harvest. But Jesus told His disciples at Sychar that they would only be able to enjoy the glory of the harvest because countless others in generations past were willing to do "the hard work." And what is this crucial hard work to which Jesus referred?

The work of sowing.

Many of our modern churches and evangelistic movements were founded during a time when the American fields were abundantly white for harvest. But the fields of the fifties and sixties, like the fields of Jesus' time, were ripe for harvest because of countless sowers who had worked to create a soil that was conducive to the growth of the gospel. The "soil" of our society is the whole environment in which Christians seek to live and minister. It is the culture, the atmosphere, the worldview, the *zeitgeist*—the "spirit of the time" in which we live. In each generation, Christians must attempt to plant the seed of the Word of God in the soil of the prevailing culture. Historically, some soils have been better than others. In each case, the nature of the soil determines what kind of life it will support.

The simplicity and neatness of a redwood forest gives the impression that it was ordered by human hands. It wasn't. The great sequoia trees of California cover the ground beneath them with a thick bed of pine straw. As the needles decompose, they alter the acidity of the soil. Almost nothing can grow except for green, leafy ferns. Analyze the soil; the soil will tell you what will grow.

Jesus told us that ministry is like sowing seed on different kinds of soil. Some soil is thin, rocky, and choked with thorns. Some soil is rich with nutrients for growing plants. Each human life is a type of soil, with its own level of fertility to the seed of the gospel. "Good soil" is a personal worldview that makes acceptance of the gospel possible: a belief in the possible existence of a God, a belief in historical objectivity, a belief in moral absolutes, a belief in the possibility of miracles, and so on. Each of these beliefs is a kind of "nutrient" that makes the soil arable. Without all of them, belief in the gospel is virtually impossible.

There is no doubt that the soil of our society has eroded significantly in a short period of time. Over the last forty years, many parachurch organizations and churches have struggled with a thinning harvest in America. In an attempt to recapture the glory of past harvests we have recruited more harvesters, sharpened our sickles and scythes, and challenged our workers to greater commitment and longer hours.

Maybe it's time to analyze the soil. Maybe it's time to *sow*.

Sowing for the Next Harvest

Each nation as a whole has its own soil, created slowly over a period of years—perhaps generations. This is the domain of the sower, a world of millions of daily communications and interactions between people that help to create an environment where the gospel will either flourish or flounder. A constant battle goes on for the soil of the culture, a battle that is rarely recognized as such because it takes place at an evolutionary pace. It is a grand conflict, the eternal struggle, the ultimate battle—but, strangely, it has become the evangelical world's Vietnam. Instead of being recognized as the crucial ministry that it is, sowing has become an unofficial war waged by unsupported, underequipped personnel who return from daily battle unnoticed, unheralded, unworthy of the recognition due those who serve in "true ministry."

In our zeal for the harvest, we have forgotten—we have deliberately *devalued*—the role of those who sow in our generation. And why not? After all, what kind of fool would continue to sow when the harvest has arrived? Because of the evangelistic success of the last forty years, we have concluded that we have entered a state of perpetual harvest—the Last Harvest—and that the fields of our society will be forever white. In our enthusiasm we have declared harvesting to be our exclusive domain, forgetting that we have reaped the benefits of someone else's labor—the labor of sowers—and that *we are also responsible to sow, or the next generation of Christians will have nothing to reap.*

In the 1990s, scores of Christian organizations announced evangelistic efforts focused on the year 2000. In the minds of many Christians, this is not just any harvest—this is the Last Harvest. This is the fourth and final lap of the Olympic 1500-meter run, and we have started our fateful kick toward the finish line.

But what if this *isn't* the final lap?

Jesus told His disciples that one day, in heaven, both the sower and the reaper would "be glad together." But what if the sower decides not to sow? What if he decides to sit and watch? What if he decides that he would really rather harvest? What if the sower is unwilling to do the exhausting, unrewarded, behind-the-scenes work of *preparing* for the harvest?

What if the sower decides that harvesting is the only worthy form of labor? What if the harvester, by elevating the importance of his own role, devalues the role of the sower until no one can be found who will fill that second-rate role?

Answer: There will be one last harvest, and then there will be famine.

This book is about avoiding that famine.

The poet Virgil said, "Not every soil can bear all things." This book is a kind of soil analysis of the American culture at the beginning of the third millennium. It's a warning that our spiritual soil is being depleted to the point that it may soon be incapable of supporting life. It's a call to a new generation of sowers to come help reclaim our eroding soil and begin to prepare the harvest of the future. And it is a rebuke to the Christian world for *encouraging the erosion to happen.*

A Parable for Our Time

Once upon a time there was a Christian who ministered in a great country. It was not an easy country in which to minister. The people were stubborn and uncaring, like their fathers before them. They did not like to talk about God. They would not listen to the Christian, and they were embarrassed to be around him. For years the Christian prayed for them and did what he could for them, just as his father before him had done. *How I hate to minister this way,* he thought. *It takes years of work to see any results at all.*

Over time, the people began to change. The Christian had talked with them and prayed for them for so long that they were no longer uncomfortable around him. They began to think about God; they even talked about Him. They had many questions and complaints, but the Christian handled them as best he could. "How I hate these endless questions and complaints," he grumbled. "How long will I have to deal with all these problems before I can tell them what they really need to hear?"

Finally, the people were ready. Everywhere the Christian looked, people seemed willing—even eager—to hear about the gospel. The Christian could tell them what was *really important.* They listened, and they believed him, and they apologized for their stubbornness and apathy. Everywhere, people began to change. "Now this is what I have waited for!" the Christian cried. "The great harvest has come, and God has let me taste the fruits of my labor."

One day, the Christian met a man whose life had not changed. The man did not like the Christian, and he did not want to listen to him. He had many difficult questions. *Why waste my time on this person?* the Christian thought. *It will take so long to answer all of his questions, and there are so many people who are ready to listen to me now.* So the

Christian decided then and there that he would no longer answer questions or hear complaints. He would only talk to people who were ready to respond. "After all," he reasoned, "changing lives is the important thing, and every day I can see a life change."

But over time, the Christian found fewer and fewer people who seemed willing to listen to him. People began to have more questions, even harder than before. "I must not be distracted," he insisted, and he continued to look for those who were ready.

One day, the Christian could find no one at all who would listen to him. *These people's hearts have grown cold,* he thought. *These are surely the end times. I must talk to anyone else who is ready without delay.* The Christian heard of a country far away where the people were always willing to listen. *If that is where people are ready, then that is where I will go.*

So the Christian loaded his car and rolled away.

Chapter 2 | EARTHQUAKE

For several years my wife and I lived in Southern California, about a mile from the San Andreas Fault. Needless to say, earthquakes were a regular occurrence. Newcomers to the area who had never actually experienced an earthquake often envisioned elaborate contingency plans that they expected to carry out when the "big one" hit. *I'll grab all the photo albums and important papers and carry them out of the house. I'll fill the bathtub with water for emergency use. I'll get a wrench and shut off the gas at the meter. I'll guide my family out into the yard, away from trees and power lines.*

People who have actually experienced a severe earthquake have a much more modest set of expectations. The American Red Cross, in its Disaster Safety materials, recommends that you plan to do only three things in the event of a quake: Drop, Cover, and Hold On. In other words: fall down, cover your head, and grab hold of something—it doesn't really matter what, since nothing will be standing still. The grandiose plans of the inexperienced are all founded on one faulty assumption: *that there will be solid ground to stand on.*

Christians admonish one another to remain firm in the faith, to take a stand, to hold our ground—but what if it seems as if there's no solid place to stand in our culture? How do you "take a stand" if the very ground beneath your feet is in upheaval?

Eric Miller, in his book *Future Vision: The 189 Most Important Trends of the 1990s,* begins with these words:

> The world as you know it no longer exists.
> The world you will know is unlike anything you've ever seen.[1]

To put it a different way: "If you're finding it difficult to take a stand, perhaps it's because there's nothing familiar to stand on."

What kind of soil is required to support the weight of Christian belief? Consider several helpful elements:

If I believe . . .	then I will be able to believe . . .
that something exists outside the universe,	that there might be a spiritual world.
that an eternal, infinite being could exist,	that the God of the Bible could exist.
that there might be absolute truth,	that there might be such a thing as sin.
that miracles are theoretically possible,	that the Resurrection could have occurred.

Church historians have noted that the primary attack on the gospel has changed from century to century. In the eighteenth century, it's said, Truth died. In the nineteenth century, God died. As a result, in the twentieth century, Man died. Christians have often arrived at the battlefront a generation late, eager to defend the faith but equipped to counter a foe who has long since withdrawn from the front lines. A formidable new foe surprises us, armed with unfamiliar weapons, and we retreat in haste to rearm and form new strategies, only to return and repeat the process a generation later. Hindsight has a remarkable acuity; the challenge is to recognize the current foe and to anticipate his future replacement *today.*

I believe that the enemy's current plan of attack is the most insidious that Christians have ever faced. Unable to destroy our forces directly, the enemy is seeking to destroy the ground on which we stand. He is seeking—with great success—to render Christian belief *impossible*.

Consider what happens to the Christian faith when certain basic elements of our soil are depleted:

If I no longer believe . . .	**then I will believe . . .**
that history can be objectively known,	that nothing can be known about Jesus.
that words convey an author's meaning,	that the Bible can be made to say anything.
that Truth can exist,	that sin is just a cultural concept.
that a writer can escape his cultural biases,	that the Bible contains no timeless truths.

These are precisely the beliefs that are rapidly dominating our postmodern culture. The average Christian, armed with weapons designed to counter yesterday's modernist attack, finds himself frustrated and bewildered as the soil continues to melt away beneath his feet.

Not long ago, I was speaking on the campus of North Carolina State University. At a busy intersection near the heart of campus, a number of student organizations had set up booths and bulletin boards announcing their causes and upcoming events. One large placard bore this message:

IT ISN'T WRONG TO THINK YOU'RE RIGHT,
BUT IT ISN'T RIGHT TO THINK OTHERS ARE WRONG

At first glance, it appeared to be a noble sentiment. "Don't be arrogant," it seemed to say. "It's fine to have your own convictions, but allow others the dignity and freedom to formulate their own." How *tolerant*.

But the more I thought about the message, the more it reminded me of one of Jack Handy's tongue-in-cheek "Deep Thoughts":

Instead of having "answers" on a math test, they should just call them "impressions," and if you got a different "impression," so what, can't we all be brothers?

How can I believe that something is right, I wondered, *and at the same time believe that the person who disagrees with me is also right?* Two plus two is four—I believe that. But in believing that, I also believe that all those who arrive at any other sum are *mistaken.* In many cases, to believe that you are right is *by definition* to believe that those who disagree with you are wrong.

How *intolerant.*

For those unaware of the changing soil in America, sentiments like the one on the campus placard appear harmless and even admirable. But to a soil analyst, they represent a major change in the atmosphere in which Christians must live and work.

America's Disintegrating Soil

An associate of mine at the Communication Center was once invited to speak on behalf of a Christian organization in New York City. The sponsoring group arranged for him to give a "free speech" in Washington Square Park. It was the Fourth of July weekend, and the park was jammed with every kind of being imaginable. Huddles of shirtless teenagers played hackey-sack. Aspiring astrologers wandered through the crowd calling, "When were you born? I'll do your sign for you." A throng of more spirited citizens encircled a man burning an American flag. My friend noticed one man walk by a park bench and drop a handful of crumpled bills. A split second later a second man scooped up the bills and left in its place a small plastic bag. Almost instantly, a third man snatched up the plastic bag and disappeared into the crowd. Just another day at the park.

It was time to begin. The sponsor of the Christian group did the introduction. Stepping up onto a small platform, he announced through his bullhorn, "We're a group of Christians from all over the United States. We'd like to share with you how you can have a personal relationship with Jesus Christ."

A collective groan rose from the audience. Not *again.* Not one of *those* guys. Three of New York City's finest, hearing the bullhorn, approached the speaker. "You can't use that bullhorn without a permit," they announced in front of the groaning congregation.

Instantly, the audience erupted in applause.

Washington Square Park that day was a microcosm of the United States itself. Every age group, every ethnic group and class were represented. Every social custom, manner, fashion, and hairstyle could be observed. A dozen languages were spoken; a score of political and social causes were discussed; every major vice and virtue was demonstrated. No one raised an eyebrow. A group happily encircled a smoldering American flag as though it was a campfire. No problem! Small bags of "controlled" substances changed hands everywhere. That's life. Banners and posters called for commitment to the most bizarre fringe groups. Welcome to America. In fact, in all of Washington Square Park, only one small group seemed to merit the anger and derision of the audience.

The Christians.

For years, Christians have enjoyed a "favored nation" status within our culture. This is largely because, due to our numbers and influence, we have virtually created the cultural soil on which we stand. That soil is changing. Christians are just beginning to wake up to the growing impatience, animosity, and even open hostility our culture now shows to Christians.

It could get worse.

America has always been known as a diverse culture, but today the melting pot boils more hotly than ever before. Consider a few statistics about our increasingly diverse society:

- 32 million Americans—14 percent of the population—speak a language other than English as their primary language in the home.[2]

- As of April 1998, 25.8 million U.S. residents, or 9.7 percent of the population, had been born in foreign nations—the highest percentage since 1930.[3]

- In the 1960s, immigration accounted for 16 percent of the U.S. population growth. Within a single generation, immigration will account for almost *half* of all U.S. population growth.[4]

With our growing ethnic diversity comes religious diversity and the awkwardness it brings to Christianity's claims to uniqueness. In the seventeenth and eighteenth centuries, the church felt this struggle for the first time as the printing press brought an avalanche of information about the world's religions and philosophies to the Christian's front door. Today, the religions *themselves* have arrived at the front door. If it was awkward in 1700 to say that "Jesus is the only way" in the light of new knowledge about Islam, what is it like for the Christian today to make that claim when the family next door is Muslim?

From the Many, One?

New Testament scholars William Crockett and James Sigountos express the growing tension that Christians feel.

> Today, a growing number of Christians are abandoning the tradi-
> tional teaching that salvation is found in Christ alone. They look
> around and see thousands of millions of people—good people from
> other lands with other faiths—who had no opportunity to hear the
> gospel. They wonder about the Ethiopian mother who carried her
> children across barren lands, looking for milk and bread, until her
> sickly body collapsed in exhaustion. They ask about those who die
> clutching amulets or religious fetishes, praying for release from their
> misery. Are we to suppose, they ask, that our merciful God simply
> translates these wretched people from one hell to another?
>
> How do evangelicals handle such challenges? The truth is, not very
> well.[5]

America prides itself on its rich cultural diversity. But our real pride is in the fact that, despite all of our differences, we are able to live together in peace and harmony. *E Pluribus Unum,* "from the many, one" the motto on our coinage reads. Many cultural observers fear that a more contemporary motto might be "From the one, many." Our nation has splintered into a thousand competitive spe-cial-interest groups. Diversity continues to increase while peace and harmony decline. Modern America has been called "a mosaic with-out cement."

To resist the growing anger, prejudice, and division in our society, we remind ourselves that this is a pluralistic society. "Pluralistic" literally means "a condition of society in which numerous distinct ethnic, religious, or cultural groups coexist within one nation." But we mean much more when we say we are pluralistic. After all, Bosnia, Rwanda, and Northern Ireland are all pluralistic nations. We're talking about an attitude *toward* our differences.

In philosophy, pluralism is "the belief that no single explanation or view of reality can account for all the phenomena of life." This comes much closer to what we use the word to mean. Modern Americans believe more deeply and passionately than ever that *no one* has a monopoly on truth. Every philosophy, every religion, every social and political group makes a contribution to our understanding of life.

Two elderly culture watchers were once ruminating on the changing face of America. The first one sighed, "Well, it takes all kinds to make a world." The second grumbled, "It don't *take* all kinds. We just *got* all kinds." Modern Americans vehemently disagree with the second man. It *takes* all kinds.

Pluralism and Tolerance

Pluralism as we mean it today is made possible by her twin sister, Tolerance. Tolerance is the cement that keeps the cultural mosaic from crumbling into a thousand fragile tiles. But the mosaic is growing larger and weightier; the cement needs to be stronger. As the diversity of America increases, so does our emphasis on the need for tolerance.

But what *is* this superglue capable of binding together all the myriad pieces of the national puzzle? The word "tolerance" simply means "sympathy or indulgence for beliefs or practices differing from or conflicting with one's own." By definition, to tolerate someone implies that you do not agree with his views. You're simply willing to *indulge* him.

Dr. John Gray of Oxford University makes the point even more strongly.

> [Tolerance] is unavoidably and inherently judgmental. When we tolerate a practice, a belief, or a character trait, we let something be that

we judge to be undesirable, false, or at least inferior; our toleration expresses the conviction that despite its badness, the object of toleration should be left alone. This is in truth the very idea of toleration, as it is practiced in things great and small. So it is that our tolerance of our friends' vices makes them no less vices in our eyes: rather, our tolerance *presupposes* that they are vices.[6]

Can *this* be the tie that binds our hearts in one accord—a willingness to *put up* with each other? How can Republicans and Democrats ever live in true harmony if Republicans believe that the political philosophy of Democrats is *mistaken?* No, modern Americans say, mere indulgence is no longer enough. In troubled times we need a stronger glue.

In the 1940s, rabbi and author Joshua Liebman offered this definition for tolerance: "Tolerance is the posture and cordial effort to understand another's beliefs, practices, and habits without necessarily sharing or accepting them." Today, Liebman's definition has come to be known as "negative tolerance." It has been angrily rejected in favor of a more open-minded "positive tolerance," which could be defined this way: "Tolerance is the posture and cordial effort to understand another's beliefs, practices, and habits, *and to accept them as equally valid approaches to life.*" It is no longer enough to simply understand. Today, to be merely *tolerant* is to be *intolerant.*

In 1994, Christian Leadership Ministries, a ministry of Campus Crusade, began a media campaign on college campuses called "Every Student's Choice." The campaign was intended to increase student awareness of Christianity and its relevance to student life and struggles. A series of full-page advertisements was created to run in student newspapers. Each one focused on a different campus issue. In February, during "National Condom Week," the ad featured a photograph of a variety of condoms. The headline said, "Too bad they don't make one for your heart." During Easter week the ad displayed the images of Alexander the Great, Pharaoh Tutankhamen, and Julius Caesar. The caption said: "They conquered everything . . . but death." In February, during Black History Month, the headline announced, "Jesus Christ died for the sins of one race: the human one." Each ad offered a phone number to call for further information. The series was extremely well received, and Christian Leadership was inundated with requests for further information.

Then Christian Leadership decided to run two ads addressing gay and lesbian students. One ad featured a photograph of a young man named Alan who had come out of the gay lifestyle. "Even though I kept going back to gay bars," the headline announced, "I knew God loved me. He was there with me, waiting." The second ad featured Anne, a former lesbian. "As a lesbian," her story began, "I found hurt people just wanting someone to love. As a Christian, I found loving people just wanting to heal my hurt."

The response to the ads was immediate and indignant. Northern Illinois University threatened to revoke the student charter of Campus Crusade unless the ads were withdrawn. The University of Washington attempted to force the local Campus Crusade movement to include gay students among its officers. Georgia Tech and other universities tried to ban the ads. At the University of Virginia, gay students posted a flier across campus that read:

Kampus Krusade for Krist?
Last Thursday, the Campus Crusade for Christ ran an ad insulting and attacking UVa's gay students. The ad suggested gays have absent or uncaring fathers, sexually abuse children, become gay through sexual abuse, are "desperate for male affection," have low self-esteem, are irreligious and promiscuous, recruit people to gay life, become gay by choice, and can be "cured" if only they would turn to God. The ad insulted all gay students, faculty and staff, their friends and family, and anyone who disapproves of irrational hate—and should not have been run by the Cavalier Daily.
Cruelty, Hate and Dishonesty are not Christian Values!

What had Christian Leadership done wrong? The tone of the ads was gracious and gentle. Each one spoke of God's love and a caring, waiting Christian community. How could *anyone* object to such a message?

Each ad closed with the words, "There is another way out." But why should anyone *want* out? By offering a way out of the gay lifestyle—*any way at all*—Christian Leadership had implied that there was something *wrong* with the gay lifestyle; that, in some way, it might be *inferior* to a heterosexual lifestyle. Christian Leadership had committed the unpardonable sin.

They were tolerant—but only by the first definition.

Stephen Carter, Professor of Law at Yale University, describes this unpardonable sin in his book *The Culture of Disbelief.*

> One good way to end a conversation—or start an argument—is to tell a group of well-educated professionals that you hold a political position (preferably a controversial one, such as being against abortion or pornography) because it is required by your understanding of God's will. In the unlikely event that anyone hangs around to talk with you about it, the chances are that you will be challenged on the ground that you are intent on imposing your religious beliefs on other people. And in contemporary political and legal culture, nothing is worse.[7]

In our contemporary culture, Carter says, *nothing* is worse than an attempt to impose your religious beliefs on someone else. Why? Because an attempt to persuade someone else to your position presupposes that you believe his position to be flawed or inferior. All attempts to persuade are judgmental. They are, by modern redefinition, intolerant—and greeted with anger. Samuel Taylor said, "I have seen gross intolerance shown in the support of tolerance."

The New Tolerance and Evangelism

In June of 1996, 13,700 delegates met at the annual Southern Baptist Convention at the Superdome in New Orleans. There they adopted a resolution to place a greater emphasis on evangelizing Jews. The resolution was widely publicized by the national press. Jewish leaders responded to the resolution with outrage. The head of the American Jewish Congress called it "offensive doctrinal arrogance"; on national television one rabbi termed the effort "spiritual genocide."

Genocide? By using that word, the rabbi recalled to collective memory the Holocaust and Hitler's attempt to exterminate the Jewish people. Imagine the chagrin of the Southern Baptists. They thought they had passed a simple resolution to bring the good news of God's love to God's people. Instead, their intention was viewed as the genocidal edict of the spiritual Gestapo. As Stephen Carter said, *nothing is worse.*

The new tolerance has created a tremendous ethical and emotional tension for Christians. On the ethical level, what are we to do with Christ's claims to uniqueness? Jesus said, "I am the way, and the truth, and the life; no one comes to the Father but through Me" (John 14:6). Do we disagree with Him? How much can we "adjust" our understanding of His words before they are no longer His words at all? Can we believe that Jesus is the Truth and at the same time believe that all contradictory claims are also true? Jesus said to the woman caught in adultery, "Neither do I condemn you. . . . Go now and leave your life of sin" (John 8:11 NIV). Did His very offer of forgiveness presuppose an intolerant judgment of the woman's lifestyle? Is *the gospel itself* "offensive doctrinal arrogance"?

Can a Christian be a Christian without being intolerant?

On an emotional level, there is an even greater tension. Christians for centuries have viewed themselves as tolerant people. It's certainly true that throughout history terrible and intolerant things have been done in the name of Christ—just as terrible and intolerant things have been done in the name of love, truth, justice, and freedom. But certainly those are examples of people acting inconsistently with Christ's words. Christianity itself is a paragon of tolerance. "There is neither Jew nor Greek, there is neither slave nor free man, there is neither male nor female; for you are all one in Christ Jesus," Paul wrote (Galatians 3:28). All who would may come. God is not a respecter of persons. The one who comes to Him He will certainly not cast out.

But suddenly, Christians find themselves cast in the role of the bigot, the faultfinder, the censor, the religious elitist—the intolerant. In university classrooms, Christianity is often represented as a model of arrogance and insensitivity. Millions of well-meaning Christians, whose gracious message and loving motives have never changed, have awoken to find that *we are the bad guys.* The emotional impact is incalculable. "I imagine," Woodrow Wilson said, "that it is just as difficult to do your duty when men are sneering at you as it is when men are shooting at you."

Can a Christian be a Christian and still be a good guy?

The message from our culture is growing louder: If the world is to become a true global village, if liberals and conservatives are to overcome their ideologies and work together, if our nation is to celebrate its rich cultural and ethnic diversity, then we must eliminate those things—and those teachings—that divide us. America can no longer afford to tolerate the intolerant.

America can no longer afford the gospel.

Unstable Ground Beneath Our Feet

A cultural earthquake is under way. Sincere Christians, fully intending to make a stand for their beliefs, are finding that they are able to do little more than drop, cover, and hold on until the ground stops shaking. It's a difficult time to be a confessing Christian—and in our increasingly diverse and "tolerant" society, *it could become much more difficult.*

The earthquake we're experiencing is not the result of seismic forces. Our shifting soil has been created by generations of secular artists, poets, philosophers, and writers who slowly changed the nature of the ground on which we stand. They have sown the cultural wind, and we are reaping the whirlwind.

What can we do? Those of us in harvesting positions—church and parachurch workers—must rethink our concept of "true ministry." We have come to believe that there are only two kinds of Christians: the harvesters and the disobedient. We must begin to teach, with great urgency, that every Christian everywhere is a *laborer.* We must tell Christians that every laborer *should* learn to reap, and that God will call some to exercise this role exclusively—but everyone can learn to sow right now, right where they are.

In short, we must revalue the role of the sower. We must encourage a new generation of Christian sowers that their work matters to God, that we are true partners in ministry, and that the fate of future harvests depends on their efforts. If we are harvesters, instead of endlessly exhorting them to join us in *our* role of harvesting, we must equip them to fulfill *their* role, a role that God has given them, so that one day the sower and the harvester can be glad *together.*

The wisest man who ever lived told us that there is a time for everything, and a season for every activity under heaven. There is a time to reap and there is a time to sow.

It's time to sow.

Chapter 3 | CALLING DOWN FIRE

I n the fall of 1975 I was actively involved in the ministry of Campus Crusade for Christ at Indiana University. At one of the weekly meetings, the campus director unexpectedly announced that there would be no presentation that evening. Instead, we were all going to pair up and go out on campus to find someone with whom to "share our faith."

This announcement was met with the same enthusiasm as if he had announced that we would all be having root canals. This was just the kind of thing one could expect from Campus Crusade. One of their core principles is that a central part of the Christian faith is a willingness to *communicate* the Christian faith. This wonderful, frightening principle changed the whole direction of my Christian life, but not before I learned a few lessons—the hard way.

We all reluctantly agreed to go and to meet back an hour later to tell our experiences. My roommate and I decided to team up, and we headed out to the streets of downtown Bloomington to look for an appropriate target. We spotted a solitary figure standing under a streetlight. He met all of our criteria: He was alone, he seemed to have nothing to do, and he was smaller than we were. We approached.

"Hi," I said, "my name is Tim, and this is Dave." I forgot to ask *his* name. "We'd like to share with you the contents of this little yellow booklet. Would that be OK with you?"

He turned and began to walk slowly away, his eyes glued to the sidewalk. He said nothing in response to our question, so we assumed his consent. I began to read.

"This first page says that, just as there are laws that govern the physical universe, so there are spiritual laws that govern our relationship with God . . ."

I plunged ahead. As I finished each of the four Spiritual Laws, I was careful to stop and add an illustration or explanation. For his part, he said nothing; he simply began to pick up the pace of his walk, his eyes never leaving the ground before him.

"Man is sinful and separated from God, so we cannot know Him personally or experience His love." We came to an intersection. Without waiting for the light to change, he darted across. We were right behind him, reading fast.

"Jesus Christ is God's only provision for man's sin. Through Him alone we can know God personally and experience His love." By this time, we were almost at a dead run. What a sight we must have been: one student running down the sidewalk with two others in hot pursuit, reading as they went, like some sort of mobile study group.

We arrived at his dormitory just as I finished my presentation. He was out of sidewalk, I was out of Laws, and we were all out of breath. He flung open the front door, then wheeled around and looked at us for the first time. His glare was a presentation in itself.

"*Thank* you," he said sarcastically. "You have just repeated to me everything that I had to listen to for eight years of Catholic school!" The door slammed behind him.

Dave and I looked around sheepishly, wondering if anyone had seen us clearly enough to identify us. We began the long, long walk back to the meeting place, dreading the upcoming "opportunity" to tell the other students the story of our profound spiritual encounter. I could hear the other students' stories now: the lonely freshman from a broken home who received the gospel in tears; the alcoholic pre-med student who not only came to faith but became sober instantly; the impromptu testimony given at a drunken fraternity party, which ended with all the brothers joining hands and singing "How Great Thou Art." Then it would be *our* turn. "We read a tract at one guy," we would say. "He tried to run away, but we stayed right with him. He yelled at us, but he didn't actually throw anything. We're not sure, but we think he'll be enrolling in seminary this fall."

For a long time, as we walked we said nothing. Then we began the all-important, highly imaginative process of rationalizing away the disaster that had just occurred.

"Well, I'm glad we did that," I ventured.

Dave spoke up—for the first time, the little weasel. "Me, too. You know, the Bible says that God's Word never returns void."

Void. What I felt deep inside, where my soul used to be.

"That's right," I replied. "There's no telling what *actually* took place here tonight. Who knows what that guy might be thinking right now?" We both had a pretty good idea, but this was certainly not the time to bring it up.

We took turns offering different interpretations of our encounter, each one more solemn, more spiritual, more inventive than the last. We had *sowed seed* here tonight—who knows when it might bear fruit? We had *stepped out in faith,* and we would have to leave the results to God. We had *opened a conversation* with this student, and some future friend or roommate would have to finish it for us.

I saved my very best, most spiritual spin for last . . .

"The most important thing," I said solemnly, "is that we did what *we* were supposed to do. What *that* guy does with the message is up to *him.*"

It's difficult to describe the impact this last perspective had on us. Suddenly, we felt that we had joined the company of ancient prophets and martyrs. We had dared to boldly name the Name, only to be despised and rejected. Jesus *said* that if the world hated Him, it would hate us also. Tonight this prophecy had been fulfilled in our midst. But did we shrink back? No. That student would *answer* one day for his response. Never mind; *we* had done what *we* were supposed to do.

We walked into the meeting hall with a new sense of dignity and importance. We had found a way to present our experience with honor and self-respect. It was no small feat—we had found a way to make a plane crash look like a scheduled part of the air show. Most important, we had convinced ourselves that we had fulfilled our duty as faithful witnesses of our Savior.

So why is it that, deep inside me, a voice seemed to say over and over, *"You have your reward in full"*?

Focusing Correctly

Anyone who has regularly attempted "random" evangelism—walking up to a complete stranger and initiating a conversation about spiritual issues—knows that wonderful things can result. Campus Crusade's insistence on encouraging young believers to tell of their faith had a profound impact on my Christian experience, and it's the reason I'm a part of their staff today.

Campus Crusade wanted me to talk to that student—*but not that way.* It takes no great insight to spot a dozen foolish blunders in my approach: the failure to ask his name; the failure to ask any questions about him at all; the failure to seek his express consent to listen to me; the failure to pick up subtle, telltale signals that might suggest his disinterest (like the fact that he was running away as fast as he could). All of my blunders resulted from one fundamental error: To me, the student was only a "target." He was there to help me fulfill my obligation and return to my friends with a story to tell. He was there to serve my ends. I was communicating a message that could change his life, but *it was all about me.*

The Value of Moral Courage

One of the qualities that Christians have always valued greatly is moral courage: the willingness to take a stand, to do the right thing, to stand up and testify. No wonder. A full hundred-and-fifty years after the apostolic age, Christians still accounted for less than 2 percent of the population of the Roman Empire. Christianity is used to being a minority worldview, and it has frequently found itself in an adversarial relationship with the prevailing culture. Historically, the Christian's anatomy has required a stiff backbone to support it, and church history abounds with stories of the great cloud of witnesses who stayed faithful to the sometimes dreadful end.

We thrill to stories of the moral courage of others, and we repeat these stories to one another to strengthen our own resolve. We tell of Telemachus, the fourth-century monk who, visiting the Roman Coliseum for the first time, was appalled to realize that men were about to destroy one another for the entertainment of the audience. He leapt into the arena and shouted, "In the name of Christ, forbear!" A gladiator cut him down with a single blow. Yet Telemachus's courage galvanized the opponents of the circus, and that was the last gladiatorial contest ever held in the Coliseum.

We tell of Martin Luther, who stood before the Diet of Worms and proclaimed, "Here I stand! I can do no other." We tell of Sir Thomas More, the "Man for All Seasons," who chose death rather than surrender his integrity to Henry VIII. We tell of the burning of Jan Hus, the execution of Dietrich Bonhoeffer. Church history is one long tutorial in the virtue of moral courage.

A quick survey of Christian children's literature shows that moral courage is one of the qualities we most want to cultivate in the next generation. Books and Sunday school materials for our youngest readers feature Moses confronting Pharaoh, David facing up to Goliath, and Daniel & Company facing off with the entire Babylonian Empire. You're not likely to find an Illustrated Golden Classic featuring the apostle Paul "becoming all things to all men, that he might by all means win some."

The Limitations of Moral Courage

Our youth ministries are sometimes built around this virtue. The ultimate goal is to "challenge" our young people, to "stretch" them. I once spoke with a high school youth group leader who was about to challenge his students to go to a busy downtown intersection and do "street preaching." It was the most intimidating (and potentially humiliating) experience he could think of, so it represented the ultimate test of courage. The whole project suggested an "I dare you" mentality. "So you think you're willing to stand up for Christ? I dare you to try *this*."

I asked the youth group leader if he thought street preaching was the most effective way to communicate the gospel to the urban community. He looked at me as though I had asked a question about

French cooking. What does that have to do with anything? This is all about *faith*. This is all about *convictions*.

This is all about *us*.

Love and Justice in Proper Balance

Twenty years ago, Wheaton College professor Em Griffin wrote a book entitled *The Mind Changers: The Art of Christian Persuasion*. He argued that whenever a Christian attempts to persuade an unbeliever, the Christian has two requirements: the requirement of love and the requirement of justice.[1]

Love requires the Christian to ask questions like these:

• What does this person most need from me right now?
• How can I bring about the greatest possible good in his life?
• What will be the short-term effect on him if I attempt to communicate in this way? What might be the long-term residual effect?

Justice has a different set of requirements. Justice requires the Christian to ask questions like these:

• What does God expect of me in this situation?
• What ought I to do or say?
• What is the right thing for me to say, regardless of this person's response?

Griffin argued that an ethical (and effective) Christian persuader must always seek to balance the requirements of love and justice. That's easier said than done. In practice, love and justice sometimes seem to represent conflicting interests. Justice told me that I ought to speak to that solitary Indiana student. I ought to tell him about the gospel, regardless of his response. But love should have told me that he was not ready to hear it, and that my insistence might even render him unwilling to ever hear it again. What do I do? Listen to the voice of love or justice? Speak or hold my tongue?

In reality, love and justice are not competing voices, like a couple of fiercely independent lobbyists, each looking out only for his

own interests. They are more like two ambassadors who both represent the kingdom of God, each reflecting and emphasizing a different part of their Lord's will. My duty is to listen to both ambassadors
and then arrive at a decision that will be most pleasing *to their Master.*
Sometimes my decisions will seem to favor love, and sometimes they
will favor justice. Their Master will never be pleased to learn that I
have blatantly disregarded either one of them. Always, my decision
will represent the best compromise between the two that I can
imagine. Justice tells me I ought to speak to the student; I speak. But
as I press on, I sense that he is disinterested, maybe even hostile to my
message; I back off. I pursue justice in a loving way.

Jesus' Focus on the Needs of Love

In John 16, Jesus was speaking to His disciples in the upper
room. Time was short, Jesus' betrayal was at hand, and His opportunity to teach His disciples would soon be over. This was His last
chance to get in any last-minute words of exhortation or encouragement. Yet in verse 12, Jesus said, "I have many more things to say to
you, but you cannot bear them now." You can hear the voices of both
love and justice in a single sentence. "I have many more things to say
to you," said justice, "but you cannot bear them now," said love. Jesus
said what He could, then backed off.

I have often marveled at Jesus' words. Near the end of His ministry, Jesus found that He still had *many more* things that He wanted
to communicate to His disciples. But His knowledge of their mental,
physical, and spiritual condition told Him that He should stop. To go
farther would not be in their best interest. It would accomplish
nothing, from God's perspective, and in the long run could even be
counterproductive. He resisted the temptation to simply unload the
whole wagon, to just have His say. Could the disciples survive without those additional words of wisdom? Had anything critical been
left unsaid? What faith in the sovereignty of the Father!

If they had been *my* disciples, I would have said, "I have many
more things to say to you, *so listen up.* Time is short, so try to pay attention. This is important!" Three hours later I would have finished,
with the disciples looking like deer staring into headlights, and I
would have walked out saying to myself, "Well, *I* did what *I* was supposed to do. What *they* do with the message now is up to *them*." This

would have been about *me*. I would have left self-satisfied and self-vindicated, but God's purposes would not have been served.

Day in and day out, the tension between love and justice is exhausting to maintain. It requires wisdom, sensitivity, self-restraint, and faith in the sovereignty of God. I think many Christians tire of this tension and simply defer to one extreme or the other. Some act exclusively out of love. They think *only* of the other person, and justice is never allowed to prod them to do the right thing, the hard thing. Others act exclusively out of justice. They simply say what they think they *should* say, regardless of its effect on the listener. Ironically, the person who seeks to act exclusively out of love is not *more* loving, he's *less*. Sometimes "love must be tough." Every parent knows that sometimes love requires you to do the right thing, the hard thing, regardless of the child's response. "A God all-loving," said English poet Edward Young, "is a God unjust." Similarly, the person who seeks to act *only* out of justice becomes less just. Loving the other person and caring about her long-term welfare is something I *ought* to do. Justice requires love; love involves justice. Either extreme is an error—an equal error.

Our Preference for Justice

Today, Christians find themselves in the frustrating position of living in a post-Christian society. We feel like a definite minority within an increasingly hostile culture, as so many of our Christian predecessors did. But unlike our predecessors, we are keenly aware that in the recent past we seemed to be a majority. We grieve the loss of our majority status, and we respond with all the hurt and anger of a rejected lover. Christians often speak and write as though something has been taken from us that must be reclaimed; an insult has been made that must be answered; ground has been lost that must be regained; a wrong has been done that must be made right. The majority culture has taken a hostile stance, and we must answer in kind.

We are not the only ones who feel left out. "The immigrants of today," wrote columnist William Booth in the *Washington Post,* "are driving a demographic shift so rapid that within the lifetimes of today's teenagers, *no one ethnic group—including whites of European descent—will comprise a majority of the nation's population*"[2] (italics added).

No one feels like the majority. Every ethnic, political, and religious group feels like an oppressed minority, outnumbered and out-gunned, that must fight for its rights or be pushed to the back of the bus. As a result, our culture as a whole has taken on an adversarial at-titude. We are *all* oppressed, we are *all* under attack, we must *all* fight back.

Georgetown University linguistics professor Deborah Tannen describes modern America as the "Argument Culture." In her book by that title she wrote:

> The argument culture urges us to approach the world—and the people in it—in an adversarial frame of mind. It rests on the assump-tion that opposition is the best way to get anything done....
>
> The war on drugs, the war on cancer, the battle of the sexes, politi-cians' turf battles—in the argument culture, war metaphors pervade our talk and shape our thinking. Nearly everything is framed as a bat-tle or game in which winning or losing is the main concern. These all have their uses and their place, but they are not the only way—and often not the best way—to understand and approach our world.[3]

In recent years, evangelical Christians have eagerly joined the argument culture. How can we resist? There isn't simply a war on cancer going on—there's a battle for the Bible, a war between good and evil, and a struggle for the souls of men. How can we refuse to fight the good fight? After all, the Scriptures themselves tell us to think of ourselves as soldiers and boxers.

The problem is that we have so immersed ourselves in this ad-versarial attitude that we often come to regard as enemies the very people we are supposed to love. "For our struggle is not against flesh and blood," Paul reminded us, "but against the rulers, against the au-thorities, against the powers of this dark world and against the spiri-tual forces of evil in the heavenly realms" (Ephesians 6:12 NIV).

Not so. Haven't you heard? There is a war going on, and you're either *for* us or *against* us. Christians today seem to have concluded that the vast majority of Americans are against us, and so we have adopted an adversarial style of communication that becomes a self-fulfilling prophecy: We *believe* they are enemies; we *speak* to them as enemies; they *become* enemies.

John Woodbridge, professor of church history at Trinity Evan-gelical Divinity School, wrote an article entitled "Culture War Casu-

alties: How Warfare Rhetoric Is Hurting the Work of the Church."
Woodbridge believes that when Christians join the argument culture, when we take on a warlike mind-set and communication style,
it creates several problems:

- When we speak in the language of war it makes it harder for
  us to love our enemies because it inflames our own angry
  feelings.

- A war mind-set is an "us or them" mentality. There is no room
  for middle ground or nuanced positions.

- The language of war makes even the gospel itself sound like
  angry criticism instead of good news offered in love.

- When we speak in the language of war we create the impression that *we* are the true enemies—and even the aggressors.[4]

War is a time of duty. In time of war, Justice has the only voice:
What must I do? Where do I sign up? What sacrifice must I make?
Love must wait to speak until the armistice—or better, until the un-
conditional surrender. In wartime I do what I *must* do, whatever I
have the power to do, without regard for the long-term effect it
might have on my enemy. The South can be reconstructed, Europe
can be restored; right now the goal is victory.

War is also about moral courage. "In war," Woodbridge warned,
"there is no room for question or hesitation, and those who are slow
to march in lockstep seem to be cowards or traitors." What happens
when the youth group leader lays out the challenge to his high
school students to march downtown, step up on a soapbox, and begin to preach? What does he think of the student who hesitates, who
isn't sure this is the best way to communicate, who is concerned
about the effect this might have on his listeners? He isn't necessarily
a traitor; he might simply be a coward.

And war is very much about *time*. Our side has definite limits to
its manpower, matériel, and will to fight. In every war, there is a time
when it becomes clear that this is the final battle, the great invasion,
the last-ditch effort into which we must hurl every resource. Bind up
the wounded, beat the plowshares into swords; there will be *no second
chance*.

The Risks in an Unbalanced Focus

And so we return to the Last Harvest. Three beliefs have come together today in the Christian mind that threaten to burn over our spiritual landscape: our culture-war mentality that gives justice priority over love, the preeminent value we assign to moral courage, and our certainty that these are the end times.

Justice for All

Our war mentality leads us to adopt a confrontational style of communication with unbelievers. We assume their hostility in advance. The unbeliever is not a seeker to be wooed and won, but an attacker to be repelled. The Bible is no longer a love letter to the lost; it's the gospel bomb that destroys the enemy stronghold. When Christians no longer believe that the unbeliever will even *listen,* there is nothing left to do but testify. *I'll* say what *I'm* supposed to say, regardless of the effect it has on you.

Every Christian knows that the gospel is a two-edged sword. It's a message of salvation to everyone who believes, but a message of condemnation to those who willfully resist. Christians today seem convinced that in this hardened, unbelieving society we are largely communicating in the second sense. Like the prophets of old, we are announcing justice—God's impending judgment—and our communication style reflects our message. The prophet cares nothing about the audience's response. He does not persuade or reason—the time for that is past—he simply proclaims.

We find a certain satisfaction in calling down fire on our opponents. The disciples displayed a hearty willingness to serve God in this way. We should not forget the Lord's response: "But He turned and rebuked them, and said, 'You do not know what kind of spirit you are of; for the Son of Man did not come to destroy men's lives, but to save them'" (Luke 9:55–56a).

More and more Christian attempts at communication with unbelievers appear self-focused. A Christian college student literally runs down his unbelieving listener in an attempt to make sure he completes his presentation. A youth group leader sends his students to do street preaching without any thought of the effect it will have on the listeners. A man sits at a major league baseball game, draping a banner over the outfield wall that proclaims "JOHN 3:16." Never mind that the majority of Americans have no idea how to look up this reference or to what it even refers.

In each case we need to ask, "Do you believe this is the most effective way to communicate your message? Did you ask yourself, 'What short- and long-term effect will this effort have on my listeners?' Did you act out of love, or only out of justice? Do you care about *them*—or is this mostly about *you?*"

Remember Deborah Tannen's description of the argument culture: "Nearly everything is framed as a battle or game in which winning or losing is the main concern. *These all have their uses and their place,* but they are not the only way—and often not the best way . . ." (italics added). Tannen is not claiming that all attempts at argument are misguided—on the contrary. There are real battles out there, in which a war mentality is completely appropriate. But who are we at war *with,* and just how big *is* the enemy force?

John Woodbridge believes that the reconnaissance reports of enemy troop strength have been greatly exaggerated. "There are theaters of cultural warfare," he writes, "but millions of Americans are not self-consciously enlisted soldiers in them. . . . It would be wrong to confuse those in the muddled middle with the left-wing extremists." In our attempt to number the enemy forces, Woodbridge says we have inadvertently included large numbers of neutral civilians.

But wait. Is there such a thing as a "neutral civilian" in a spiritual battle? Didn't Jesus say, "He who is not with Me is against Me" (Matthew 12:30)? Indeed He did, but He also said, "He who is not against us is for us" (Mark 9:40). These two paradoxical statements of Jesus reveal that people in general can be divided into three camps:

- Those who are for us
- Those who are against us
- Those who are neither for us nor against us

This third category, Woodbridge's "muddled middle," might in different contexts support us *or* oppose us—*but they are not committed enemies.* They are the "persuadable majority" who may only be waiting to hear a message from Christians that reflects love along with justice.

Courage Above All

"Courage is not simply *one* of the virtues," wrote C. S. Lewis, "but the form of every virtue at the testing point, which means, at the point of highest reality." Courage is the willingness to hold to all of the *other* virtues—love, mercy, honesty, faithfulness—even when there is danger or personal risk. "Pilate was merciful," said Lewis, "till it became risky."[5] Courage will always be the cornerstone of all Christian virtues because courage makes all the others possible. Courage makes sure that a Christian is not just a "fair-weather friend" but a faithful servant *regardless* of the consequences. It's difficult to overestimate the value of courage in the Christian life.

Courage, in other words, was never meant to be a virtue *on its own*. When courage becomes valued for its own sake, strange things begin to happen. The American inventor Horace Smith, of Smith & Wesson fame, once remarked, "Courage is the fear of being thought a coward." Instead of being concerned that I will remain faithful, I become concerned about whether I *appear courageous*. We begin to encourage one another to gain courage instead of courageously holding to the other virtues. As Christians, we begin to make choices and choose strategies on the basis of how courageous they appear to be, rather than how good or wise or loving they might be. Ironically, this approach to courage—the fear of being thought afraid—is a form of cowardice. To rephrase Horace Smith: "Sometimes *true* courage is *resisting* the fear of being thought a coward."

We need to challenge our young people and to encourage one another as mature adults to be genuinely courageous Christians. But courage does *not* always mean walking in the path of greatest resistance or taking the greatest risk. Courage is not simply doing the most frightening, outlandish, and publicly humiliating thing. Christ said that we might be called on to appear as fools for His sake. He didn't ask for our help.

Sometimes courage is doing what you believe is the wise or loving thing, even when it is quiet or subtle or behind the scenes, even when others call you a coward for not joining them on the street corner. True courage resists the fear of being thought a coward and seeks to communicate out of love *and* justice. Sometimes, courage is *not* telling the unbeliever everything he needs to hear; sometimes, it's telling him only what he can *bear*.

No Second Chance

In 1192, during the Third Crusade, King Richard the Lion-hearted led his advancing army toward the coveted goal of Jerusalem, the Holy City. The defending general was Saladin, the Sultan of Egypt and Syria. Saladin's strategy was to employ a "scorched earth" policy; he retreated before the advancing Richard, destroying crops, salting fields, and poisoning wells. Richard soon realized that the land could no longer support his army or his horses, and he was forced to withdraw—but so was Saladin. The moral of the story is: *Never scorch the earth in a place where you must return to live.*

At the turn of the new millennium, there seems to be a heightened sense among all Christians that this is a crucial point in human history. Some see an age coming to an end as our civilization crumbles around us—we have a brief opportunity left to get in any last words. Others see a new and golden age upon us as technology creates opportunities for ministry that have never existed before—we have a brief opportunity to take advantage of the possibilities. In each case, there is a shared sense of urgency—and a resulting focus on the immediate. I believe this sense of urgency, this focus on the time immediately before us, is leading Christians to practice their own "scorched earth" policy in communicating with the unbelieving world. This is seen as a time to reap, not to sow; a time to proclaim, not to persuade.

This attitude emerges clearly when you consider our language and imagery regarding the "harvest." Jesus told us to beseech God to send out workers into His harvest. But what kind of a harvest is it? Judging by virtually every Christian book cover, poster, and church bulletin cover in existence, it's a harvest of *grain*. Vast fields of wheat have turned golden all at once, ready for the harvester's sickle.

In a wheat harvest, the grain is harvested in a short period of time. There is a small window of opportunity before weather or blight destroys the crop where it stands. Each harvester works from the beginning of the harvest to the end, and when he is finished the harvest is *done*. The reaper passes through the fields, the sheaves are bundled, the fields are cleared. A wheat harvest is a thorough, final, consummate event.

But Jesus also spoke of people as though they were a harvest of *fruit*. A fruit harvest is a very different kind of harvest—a patient, gradual, ongoing process. Though there is a harvest season, the fruit harvest takes place over a much longer period of time. It's no accident that a fruit grower is sometimes known as a "vinedresser." He can't simply walk out into the vineyard with his sickle and mow everything down. The vinedresser always enters the vineyard prepared to do a variety of jobs. He looks first for ripe fruit; where he finds none, he "dresses" the vine. He pulls a weed, fertilizes, cultivates, ties up a sagging branch. Later, a different worker may come behind him. She may find a thick, hardy vine where he tied up a feeble twig. She may find ripe fruit where he found none. No matter. At the harvest celebration, the vinedresser and the reaper will be glad together.

I believe it's crucial today for Christians to ask themselves, "What kind of a harvest do I believe this to be?" What happens when a fruit harvester is hired to harvest a wheat field? It's a comedy of errors. He wanders from stalk to stalk, examining each head of grain. The harvest will *never* get finished at that rate. But what happens when a wheat harvester is hired to work in the vineyard? It's a *disaster.* He cannot distinguish the unripe fruit from the ripe; he works too quickly to give the unripe fruit a chance to mature; he cuts down not only the fruit but the vine itself. He "scorches the earth," as it were, and he makes certain that there will be no fruit *next* year.

The majority of Christians seem to be thinking and acting as though this is a wheat harvest—and the Last Harvest at that. Time is short, we have a brief window of opportunity, we must give everyone one last opportunity to hear. Our preferred style of communication is confrontational proclamation, not gradual persuasion. We reap, but we have no time—or reason—to sow. There *is* no future harvest, and there are no workers to come after us. When we are finished, we reason, the harvest is *done.*

And if we don't sow, it will be.

A Time to Sow

I would like to suggest that, because we cannot know *for certain* that this is the Last Harvest, we must live and work as though this is a harvest of fruit. Like the vinedresser, we should enter the vineyard looking for—*anticipating*—ripe fruit to pick. That, after all, is the final goal. But we'll be careful not to bruise the fruit that's unready to pick. We'll remember that fruit harvesting is a gentle, gradual, ongoing process that requires patience and faith. The harvest is a team effort, sowers and reapers working together, and other workers will come after us. A part of *everything we do* will be for them. Seeds sown or weeds pulled are valuable, critical uses of our time, because they make the future harvest possible.

We may even begin long-term, visionary projects that we may never see come to fruition. We may negotiate to buy a whole new field. We may pull up acres of vines and let the soil lie fallow for several years. We may set aside a significant amount of time to study new techniques in horticulture. We may do any number of things that we would not do if this were *definitely* the Last Harvest.

In September of 1939 Great Britain was at war. Germany had invaded Poland, and England in turn declared war on September 3. Within a year, bombs would be raining down on London in an endless, brutal war that would ultimately take the lives of almost half a million British men, women, and children.

In the autumn of 1939, C. S. Lewis delivered a sermon entitled "Learning in War-Time" at the Church of St. Mary the Virgin at Oxford University. He spoke to a church packed with young men who, at the moment, could not remember why they were in college —not when the reality of war made everything else seem insignificant. He said,

> We have to inquire whether there is really any legitimate place for the activities of the scholar in a world such as this. That is, we have always to answer the question: "How can you be so frivolous and selfish as to think about anything but the salvation of human souls?" and we have, at the moment, to answer the additional question: "How can you be so frivolous and selfish as to think about anything but the war?"

It's interesting that Lewis said that the *first* question is one we always have to answer. Lewis felt that the war had not really introduced anything new into the equation. "What does war do to death?" he asked. "It certainly does not make it more frequent: 100 percent of us die, and the percentage cannot be increased." What war *does* do, Lewis said, is make us remember death; it makes it real to us. War simply made the first question, the timeless question, more acute: In light of the brevity of human life and the certainty of death, why should a Christian do anything other than evangelism? It's the same question we face today: In light of the end times and a decaying, post-Christian society, why should a Christian do anything other than harvest? Lewis' question is indeed timeless—and so is his answer.

"The war will fail to absorb our whole attention because it is a finite object," Lewis reasoned. The war would eventually end, and even while the war raged the world would continue to read poetry, paint paintings, and write philosophy. But he also warned, "A cultural life will exist outside the Church whether it exists inside or not." The church could not retreat from the world to pursue exclusively "sacred" activities because *the world would not make the same retreat.* "Good philosophy must exist," he reminded us, "if for no other reason, because bad philosophy needs to be answered."[6]

In light of the end times and a decaying, post-Christian society, why should a Christian do anything other than harvest? Because the world continues to sow—*and we must sow also.*

Chapter 4 | THE SOWER'S ART

Every great quotation, every poem, every story, every half-mumbled sentence, *every communication* possesses both science and art. By "science" I mean raw content, the thought or message the communicator wishes to express. I'm asked a question; I think of an answer. I'm involved in a disagreement; I prepare a response. I'm asked to explain my actions; I begin to build a logical, factual, orderly defense.

But *how* to say it—that's art. By "art" I mean the *style* of the communication: choice of words, phrasing, timing, emphasis. We are all scientists and artists. Every time we open our mouths we have something to say, and every time we speak we constantly and almost unconsciously select and arrange our words for maximum effect.

Suppose your husband seems to be a little too self-involved. You could voice your complaint with science: "I think you're conceited." Or you could communicate your observation through art: "I think the problem is that we're both in love with the same man."

Every time you choose one word over another, every time you give a moment's reflection to the turn of a phrase or the tone of your voice, you are exercising the power of art, and art can add immeasurable potency and persuasiveness to language.

This is science: "Each of us has a deep need to feel wanted." Nice thought. But you could say it in a different *way* . . .

When I lived in Southern California, the *LA Times* carried a story one day about a very ordinary four-year-old girl from a very typical Southern California family. The family was very busy, always on the go, and the little girl was often left to play by herself. She had everything she needed—except the love and attention that all four-year-olds crave.

One day the family went to a poolside barbecue and, as usual, the little girl was left to play by herself. Everything went as usual until the little girl wandered too close to the edge of the pool, slipped, and plunged in. One of the adults nearby saw her and realized in an instant that she could not swim. Immediately he dove in after her. As he pulled her, coughing and whimpering, to the edge of the pool, all of the other adults gathered around in great alarm. They wrapped her in warm blankets and soft towels, and a sea of hands stroked her arms and legs and tangled hair. "Honey, what happened?" each one cooed in turn. "Sweetheart, are you all right?" The little girl just smiled and looked up into each loving, concerned face, and in that one moment she tasted all the love and affection she had longed for all her life.

And so the little girl began to develop the habit of "accidentally" falling into swimming pools.

Each time the family attended a poolside barbecue the little girl would wander a little too close to the pool's edge, slip, and fall in. She would float face down, waiting patiently for the big soft towels and the warm loving faces to come to her rescue. She did this again, and again, and again—until the day that no one saw her fall into the pool.

They found her body thirty minutes later lying face down at the bottom.

The Coroner's death certificate listed the cause of her death as "drowning." But those who knew her—and her all-too-ordinary family—knew that she really died from something else.

She died from a lack of love.[1]

That's art.

Here's another nice thought: "It isn't enough to simply understand the teachings of Jesus—we have to apply them in our lives." It's good science; but when Jesus chose to deliver this message, He first applied some extraordinary art:

> Therefore everyone who hears these words of mine and puts them into practice is like a wise man who built his house on the rock. The rain came down, the streams rose, and the winds blew and beat against that house; yet it did not fall, because it had its foundation on the rock. But everyone who hears these words of mine and does not put them into practice is like a foolish man who built his house on sand. The rain came down, the streams rose, and the winds blew and beat against that house, and it fell with a great crash. (Matthew 7:24–27 NIV)

The Power of Art

It's no accident that "when Jesus had finished saying these things, the crowds were amazed at his teaching" (Matthew 7:28 NIV). Most of the power and persuasiveness of language come to us through art, not science. Patrick Henry left us the immortal words, "I know not what course others may take, but as for me, give me liberty, or give me death!" Would his thoughts have achieved the same longevity if he had said, "I don't care what you fellows do, I'm going to throw in with the revolution"? FDR warned us, "The only thing we have to fear is fear itself." Would his words have struck as deeply if he had said, "The biggest thing we have to worry about is our own paranoia"?

Think of the Christian ministers, authors, teachers, and speakers throughout history who have had a notable impact on their world—especially those rare few who have had an impact on the *unbelieving* world of their day. In virtually every case their impact, humanly speaking, was due to a wonderful combination of art *and* science. They were profound thinkers who were able to package their written and spoken words into beautiful, lyrical, memorable forms.

The power of art is immeasurably greater today, if for no other reason than that immeasurably more communication takes place than just a generation ago. We're overwhelmed by it, and we need some way to sort out what we will hear. Some messages grab our attention, and some don't. We're told that we live in a postmodern era;

we need to remember that postmodernism is a revolt against science, not art. Today we communicate artistically—through images and sounds—far more than through words alone. The age we live in is far more influenced by the *style* of communication than any other time in history was. It's now common to see expensive, high-tech television commercials in which the product is never directly promoted. It isn't necessary. The *images* inform, the sounds persuade. The medium is the message, Marshall McLuhan said thirty years ago, and artists have a greater opportunity for influence today than ever before.

Much has been written in the last few years about the need of the church to rethink the role of the arts in ministry. These admonitions are usually referring to the traditional arts—poetry, writing, painting, music, etc. When I use the word *art,* I'm using it in a much more general sense. Art is the style of *all* of your communication, *whatever* form it may take. Art is paying attention not only to what you say, but to how you say it. Few of us are poets, but every one of us is an artist. Some of us paint, some write, some teach, and some simply have conversations with our next-door neighbors. Every one of us is a *communicator,* and every one of us can increase our influence by developing our art.

But there's a problem. Christians don't tend to see the value of art. In this area, we are thirty years behind the rest of our culture. Christians today are far more interested in science—*what* we say— than in how we say it. What a remarkable evolution for the church that inspired and patronized some of the greatest artists of history!

Our Overreliance on Science

In the Western world since the time of the Enlightenment, there has been almost a worship of science—not the *topics* of science, like physics or botany, but the entire *methodology.* We've come to idolize logic, analysis, classification, deduction, and step-by-step processes, and this love affair has had a profound effect on our approach to the knowledge of God and the study of the Bible.

When a young person comes to Christ, he is immediately introduced to the science of the Bible. He learns that we are "transformed by the renewing of [our] mind" (Romans 12:2), and he begins to read the Bible to grow in his knowledge of God. He quickly learns that the Bible is not a book at all, but a collection of sixty-six very different books that must be studied in different ways. He learns to do book studies, character studies, and word studies. He reaches a substantial level of Christian maturity, but he still hungers to grow more. Where does he go from here? His pastor advises him that there is only one place to go—to seminary.

In seminary, he delves even further into the science of the Bible. He studies systematic theology, hermeneutical principles, and the original languages of the Scriptures. He constantly sharpens his skills of observation, interpretation, and analysis. After three or four years of intense study, he is granted a title—Master of the Knowledge of God. Unfortunately, the Master forgot something . . .

He has no art.

One typical evangelical seminary lists the following general course requirements for a Masters of Divinity degree:

Old Testament 3 courses	Social Ethics 1 course
New Testament 3 courses	Christian Education 1 course
Theology 3 courses	Ministry of the Church 2 courses
Greek 2 courses	World Missions 1 course
Hebrew 2 courses	Pastoral Counseling 1 course
Church History 2 courses	Supervised Ministry 1 course
Preaching 2 courses	

These course requirements reflect what the seminary considers necessary for a graduate to be fully equipped to have an effective ministry. Notice the relative importance given to science and art. The entire art requirement consists of two courses in Preaching and one in Christian Education, much of which may deal with content and organization and not directly with style or creative expression. The underlying assumption is clear: If a graduate is *saturated* in science and *briefly exposed* to art, he has everything he needs to make an impact on the world.

Eugene Peterson has written much about the Christian tendency to prefer "explanation" to "imagination"—to prefer science to art. "We have a pair of mental operations, imagination and explanation, designed to work in tandem," he wrote. "When the gospel is given robust and healthy expression, the two work in graceful synchronicity. . . . But our technological and information-obsessed age has cut imagination from the team."[2] Our age, he observes, is obsessed with information—and Christians share this obsession. While the entire world seems obsessed with information, the world at large is also enamored with art. The Christian community, on the other hand, does not share this joint interest; we prefer information to art. Our almost limitless technological ability to gather, store, and disseminate data has led us to become enamored with information *alone*. If we just have *enough* data, the *right* data, the problem will be solved. Here is some vital information! Photocopy it, scan it into your computer, e-mail it to your friends, post it on your Website, and the world will be changed.

Will it? Don't forget that most of the power and persuasiveness of language comes through art, not science. To put it a different way: *Information has no power to persuade or transform until it is given art.*

Philip Yancey, in his book *Open Windows,* wrote:

> When Christians attempt to communicate to non-Christians, we must first think through their assumptions and imagine how they will likely receive the message we are conveying. That process will affect the words we choose, the form and, most importantly, the content we can get across. If we err on the side of too much content, as Christians often do, the net effect is the same as if we had included no content.[3]

Information overload, or information alone, has the same impact as no information at all. Good science plus bad art equals zero impact.

The Art of the Bible

The Christian preference for science is strange indeed when you consider that our Sourcebook is a book of art. Eugene Peterson wrote, "It surprises me when pastor friends are indifferent or hostile to poets. More than half our Scriptures were written by poets."[4] When God wanted to communicate His Word to mankind He packaged His message in every literary form known to man, including poetry, narratives, parables, proverbs, and even songs.

The Christian's challenge is to understand the message; enter science. Through careful analysis and logical deduction the Christian systematically strips away the layers of art, like an archaeologist dusting away layers of useless debris, until the bones of propositional truth are revealed. Eureka! So *that's* what it means. At last, after years of applied science, the American Christian has the Scriptures as he has always wanted them—a set of orderly, step-by-step principles and propositions organized according to topic. Surely this is how God intended them, if only fuzzy-thinking human authors with their cultural conventions hadn't messed things up.

It's important that the reader not misunderstand what I'm saying. The Christian desire to understand the Bible is an excellent one, and the tools of science are essential in the process. My concern is that the average Christian believes the art of the Bible to be a useless and obscurant covering for what is of *real* value—the content. Modern evangelicals approach art the way a grade-school child approaches the gift wrapping on a present. When is the last time you saw a child on Christmas morning stop, study a package with admiration, and say, "Now *that's* a beautiful bow"? The paper is shredded in an instant as the child rushes on to the next gift. But sometimes an older and wiser parent gathers and smooths the discarded paper, thinking of how it might be used again.

When the Scriptures are unwrapped and the gift of meaning is lying exposed, the Christian thinks his task is done. Now he makes the greatest mistake of all: He takes his naked, artless set of propositions and precepts out into the world to show to others, and to his astonishment they could not be less interested. At this point the Christian has accomplished something truly remarkable, something that may have required a seminary degree. He has taken the most fascinating, life-transforming communication in the world and made it boring.

The art of the Bible is no accident. God wrapped His gift to us in magnificent and alluring paper precisely because the power and persuasiveness of language come through art—through the clever, creative, and memorable style of its delivery. Is it an accident that Psalm 23 is a poem and not a set of propositions? Is it an accident that almost 80 percent of the words in the Sermon on the Mount have only one syllable? Is it an accident that the average adult in

America knows almost nothing about Jesus but can remember at least one of His parables?

When the Christian has stripped the Bible of its art and has understood its message, her job is exactly half finished. Now she must rewrap the package to make it once again alluring and compelling to the next recipient of the gift. As she attempts to communicate and explain it to others, she must adorn her communication in the art of *her* day. *Every* Christian, even as she masters the science of the Bible, must at the same time improve her art.

In our writing, in our teaching, even in our personal conversation, we must think about how to improve the *style* of our communication. Whenever I have something to say, the artist within must always prompt me to ask, "Now *how* do I say it?"

In the last forty years both the quantity and quality of conservative Christian scholarship have exploded. Evangelicals today are able to marshal more impressive, scholarly information on behalf of our position than ever before. We now have, by *anyone's* standards, world-class philosophers, theologians, and scientists on our side. It's no exaggeration to say that evangelical Christians have experienced a literal renaissance in our science.

Unfortunately, there has been no corresponding renaissance in our art. We have more to say to our culture than ever before, and less ability to say it in a persuasive and compelling way. We are enamored with our content and cannot understand why the world isn't fascinated with our latest proofs and evidences. We insist on living as pure scientists in the age of art.

Moving Past Our Fear of Art

Our concept of the Last Harvest is one of the things that has led us to neglect the development of our art. If my focus is on justice and not love, then why should I be overly concerned with the *way* I say something? I'll say what I should say; the rest is up to the person I'm talking to.

If the most important Christian virtue is courage, then doesn't careful, artful, persuasive language appear cowardly? The most courageous thing to say is probably the most direct and the most potentially offensive. Only cowards hesitate. Are you afraid of offending someone? Take a stand!

If this is indeed the Last Harvest and we have one last chance to get our message out there, is there *time* for art? Is there time to tell a parable when we could just come right out and say what we mean? If a man is starving today, do we give him seed to plant *next* year's crop?

But art is the sower's constant concern. The sower seeks to balance love and justice, and his concern for his listener's response leads him to consider carefully the most effective manner of communication. The sower takes the long-term view, and he uses his art to sow thoughts and ideas today that could yield fruitful crops in the future —perhaps the distant future. The sower understands that he must do most of his work using language, and he wants his language to have all the power it can possess. He knows that power comes through art.

Great Art and Great Science for a Great Cause

What's really important is our ability to communicate the gospel clearly and effectively at this specific moment in history. To do that will require great art as well as great science. We know where great scientists come from—they are slowly developed through years of intensive study and discipline. But where do great artists come from? We seem to think they grow on trees. When we meet a great scholar we often say, "What a learned person," or "What an accomplished thinker." When we meet a great artist we say, "What a *gifted* person," or "What a *talented* artist," as though her skills were somehow genetically acquired. To develop an art requires every bit as much discipline, study, and application as the obtaining of knowledge—maybe more. Michelangelo was once asked how he obtained his incredible genius. "If people knew how hard I have worked to obtain my mastery," he said, "it would not seem wonderful at all."

We must begin to encourage all Christians that spiritual growth requires developing both science and art. Every Christian must grow in his knowledge of Scripture and theology, but *equally* in his ability to communicate it persuasively and attractively, whether through writing or teaching or interpersonal communication.

For this to happen, Christians will have to recognize the pursuit of art as every bit as spiritual—and as *valuable*—as the pursuit of science. For this to happen, Christians will also have to take a long-term view of ministry, because art takes a lifetime of devotion and its effects are gradual. In a word, Christians must begin to sow and to be patient to wait for the distant harvest that sowing will eventually produce.

Chapter 5 | # INDIRECT COMMUNICATION

Bevin Alexander, a British military historian and strategist, wrote a book entitled *How Great Generals Win,* in which he attempted to distill the common strategies that victorious field commanders have used throughout history. His observations are summarized this way:

> One of the remarkable facts about great generals throughout history is that—except in cases where they possessed overwhelming power—practically all their successful moves have been made against the enemy's flank or rear, either actual or psychological. Great generals realize that a rear attack distracts, dislocates, and often defeats an enemy physically by cutting him off from his supplies, communications, and reinforcements and mentally by undermining his confidence and sense of security. Great generals know a direct attack, on the other hand, consolidates an enemy's defenses and, even if he is defeated, merely forces him back on his reserves and his supplies.[1]

After studying military strategists from Hannibal to Douglas MacArthur, Alexander concluded that *all* great generals have understood and applied this principle of warfare: An indirect attack is more effective than a direct attack. Alexander observed that Napoleon "never made a frontal attack when he could do otherwise" and so conquered an entire empire. A frontal attack is too costly, it requires too many resources, and even if it's successful it only serves to push the opposing force back where it can quickly regroup for a counterattack. An indirect attack, on the other hand, is both a physical and a psychological assault. Physically it "distracts and dislocates" by cutting the enemy off from his supplies and reinforcements, and psychologically it produces terror and uncertainty. All this is accomplished not with brute force, but with subtlety, stealth, and surprise.

Indirect Spiritual Warfare

The Bible tells us that we are involved in a spiritual battle. It follows, then, that the enemy of our souls is a kind of opposing general. There is debate among Christians as to the nature and extent of Satan's powers, but it seems safe to assume that he is at least as intelligent as any human general. If all great generals know the strategy of an indirect attack, is there any reason to believe that the enemy commander in chief doesn't know and apply it as well—with equal success? In fact, this is precisely the case. While Christians man the front lines in preparation for a frontal assault, the Christian worldview is being decimated by subtle, indirect guerrilla raids on our flank and rear.

An indirect spiritual attack bypasses the listener's conscious defenses. If I attack your position directly you will recognize my attempt to persuade you, and you will almost certainly become defensive and resist me. If I can instead swing around to your flank and cut your lines of supply, I can work to destroy the beliefs and convictions that make your position *possible*. If I do this carefully—artfully—you'll never even know it happened. What *are* these indirect "guerrilla raids," and what makes them so effective?

In a current sitcom the lead character finds himself involved in a relationship based completely on sexual attraction. He can find no other likable feature about this woman except her sexual performance. He struggles with guilt—should he continue in a relationship for such a superficial reason? A friend chides him for his oversensitive conscience: "Oh come on," she says, "*everybody* has had *one!*" meaning that at some point in time everybody has had at least one relationship for purely sexual reasons. No character ever turns to the camera and addresses sexual ethics directly. There are no speeches or arguments in favor of sexual freedom. In fact, nothing is ever said *to* the listener at all; he simply *overhears* the message: "It's a normal part of life."

In another popular show, the lead characters—all single—all make a habit of sleeping with their partners at the earliest opportunity. They live in an urban area, and each has had a wide variety of sexual partners who, in turn, are sexually experienced themselves. As their relationships come and go, the characters struggle with disappointment and even heartbreak, but no one ever has an abortion, contracts genital herpes, or tests positive for HIV. The entire cast of characters has completely defied the health statistics that characterize people with their lifestyle. The producers are not claiming these things don't occur—not directly. But by completely ignoring this part of reality the show sends an indirect message: "These things rarely happen."

In a college classroom a professor presents a postmodern view of literature to his young students. "Each reader approaches a text hopelessly immersed in his own cultural viewpoints and prejudices," he explains. "Each reader, then, understands the author to mean something entirely different. There is a feminist interpretation of the text, there is a capitalist interpretation of the text—there are as many interpretations of the text as there are viewpoints. There is no way to arrive at the author's original intention. Any insistence on a single meaning of the text is simply an act of power, an attempt to force others to see life through our lenses." Nothing is ever said about the Bible or Christianity. Perhaps nobody in the class, including the professor, is even thinking about the Bible. But indirectly, the professor has removed the foundation that makes Christianity *possible*.

Understanding the Strategy of Indirect Communication

Indirect communications share three common features. First, there is no direct attempt to persuade—the real subject in question is often not even mentioned. Second, the attack is against the line of supply, some underlying belief or attitude that is critical to the support of the primary belief. Third, the style of the communication is as attractive and enjoyable as possible. Art is the chief weapon of indirect attack. Here's a brief compendium of techniques of indirect communication that you might recognize from the media:

- It is suggested that people who hold your view have emotional or character flaws.
- The most foolish or contemptible character endorses your view.
- The most desirable characters never entertain your view.
- It is suggested that people who hold your view are less intelligent or less educated.
- Your view is completely ignored, suggesting that it's irrelevant to daily life.
- A picture is created of a normal, healthy world in which your view does not exist.
- A fantasy world or future world is pictured in which your view does not exist.
- It is suggested that your view is an evolutionary step or a childish view to be outgrown.

In a direct attack, the goal is to marshal facts, to match argument with argument, to powerfully refute. The appeal is cognitive and rational, and it operates at a conscious level. An indirect attack operates at a subliminal level. Its goal is to create a *feeling* that the view in question is ignorant, foolish, childish, unsophisticated, intolerant, or any of a hundred other things that simply render the view untenable. *How* could you believe *that?*

I see the state of the spiritual battle that surrounds us this way: For the first time in many years, evangelicals have their opponents evenly matched or even outgunned on an intellectual, scientific level. We have collected impressive weaponry and personnel, and we feel prepared to mount a frontal attack or to repel any direct attack made against us. *Look at these facts. Read these proofs and evidences. Listen to our philosophers and scholars. Argue with us, debate with us, give us your best shot—we're ready for anything you can throw at us.*

But the enemy general, sensing the buildup of forces on our front lines, knows that it's no longer to his advantage to mount a frontal attack. If he attempts a major direct offensive and loses, he faces a crushing setback. But even if he *wins* a direct attack, he only pushes us back against our reinforcements; he rallies our troops and creates a sense of solidarity and unity.

To the enemy of our souls a frontal attack is currently a no-win situation, and so, while he pins down our frontline troops with minor diversionary skirmishes, his main forces have secretly, artfully swung around and are decimating our unprotected flank. Our forces have not been beaten back—our lines of supply have been cut, and we have been separated from psychological reinforcement. We still have our intellectual weaponry, but our troops are struggling with a growing subconscious sense of fear, uncertainty, and sheepishness. We haven't been proven wrong—it's worse than that. We've been shown to be *silly,* and, as one pundit has put it, "You'll never lead a cavalry charge if you think you look silly on a horse."

Our once-committed troops have begun to wander away in confusion and shame, leaving our sophisticated weapons unmanned. We wonder when the big attack will finally begin; we're completely unaware that not only has it begun, it's almost over.

Our frontline troops stand up in the trenches and shout across to the enemy, "You coward! Why don't you come out and fight like a *man?*" What we mean, of course, is "Why won't you fight *our* way? Why won't you fight science with science? We've spent years developing these weapons—why won't you give us a chance to use them? Debate us! Argue with us! Mount a frontal attack, because that's what we're ready for."

Why should he? Why should he risk a costly direct attack when he's achieving such impressive results indirectly?

An oft-repeated scenario in military history is that of a larger, better-equipped army being devastated because of its inability to adapt to the tactics of its enemy. The use of art to persuade appears to Christians as a manipulative, dishonorable way to fight, so we continue to fight only *our* way—with science, power, or withdrawal. The world produces an Oscar-nominated film in which the villain, a pathological killer, is driven by his distorted quasi-Christian views. In response, we release a book series on great men and women of faith, or we pressure the studio to halt the release of the film, or we exhort as many people as possible to refuse to go to the theater. Strangely, we seem to consider every option except for one: to make a film of our own, to answer art with art.

The obvious objection to this suggestion is, "We can't just go out tomorrow and make a film." No, we can't. Nor did our opponents begin making their film yesterday, nor did they begin learning the craft of filmmaking last week. Many of them have devoted their entire adult lives to developing a craft that they can now use with great skill to promote whatever worldview they desire. We will not be able to compete with that kind of artistry without a similar investment of time and energy—an investment that *we won't make,* because we don't value filmmaking.

You may object at this point. "Christians *do* value filmmaking. We've seen its power, and we wish we had more Christian filmmakers." To illustrate the depth of this commitment, imagine two young people appearing before the missions committee of a local evangelical church to request funding. One wants to go to seminary, the other to film school at UCLA. Who will get the funds, the scientist or the artist? "That's not fair," it might be objected, "it's a *missions* committee. It's supposed to provide funding and encouragement for those who are going into actual *ministry.*"

That's the problem. Christians continue to see spiritual growth only in terms of science and actual ministry only in terms of harvest. Art seems to be a wasteful, time-consuming distraction from What's Really Important. What's really important is that Christians learn the tactic of our enemy, the art of effective indirect communication, before it's too late. This will not be an overnight process in the evangelical community. It will require a gradual three-step process.

Learning the Art of Indirect Communication

Step 1: We must lose our fear of art and artists.

It isn't simply that we undervalue art—we fear it. Art is what happens when science gets sloppy. Art is what liberals do. Imaginative

style and creativity become ends in themselves, and the message gets
squeezed out. Good, solid expositional sermons get replaced by pup-
pet shows and interpretive dance. To be fair, that *can* happen, but it
doesn't have to. "We have such a fear of superstition and allegory,"
Eugene Peterson said, "that we squeezed all the imaginative stuff out
of Scripture so we could be sure that it was just precise and accurate.
. . . This great emphasis on how to communicate accurately is a dead-
end street. Communicating clearly is not what we're after. What we
are after is creating new life."[2] We must lose our fear of art without
beginning to worship it. Art alone is no greater virtue than science
alone. We must always work to strike a balance between the two—
clear, scriptural thinking communicated in a powerful and relevant style.

The question that must be asked is, "Where does a Christian go
to learn an art?" The answer: wherever the *world* goes to learn the
same art. This once again is where our fears come into play. We have
created unique institutions to study the science of the Bible—Bible
schools and seminaries. But because we have not valued the Christian's need to develop his *style* of communication, we have no corresponding Christian institutions to teach art. It's for the best. Art is not
a Christian topic; it's simply a human topic. There isn't one standard
of excellence for Christian writers and another standard for secular
writers; there is simply good writing and bad writing.

This is the lesson we must keep in mind: *The world sets the standard of excellence for art.* The world decides what is good and bad,
what is current and outdated, what is interesting and boring. We
must develop our art using these standards, which means that we
must learn our art alongside everyone else in the world. This is a
great fear for evangelical Christians; we would much rather create
the Christian Filmmaking Institute than risk exposing our people to
the cancerous influences of the secular world. In fact, this exposure
often brings faith to life as Christians begin to understand what the
Bible actually has to say to ordinary, unbelieving people. To face up
to these fears, the evangelical community will have to do some real
soul-searching about the relative risks and rewards of developing our
art.

Let's not be naive; there are risks to learning art alongside the
rest of the world. I attended college intending to become a sculptor.
After a brief flirtation with painting, I finally concentrated in graphic

design and spent eleven years as a professional comic-strip artist. I have seen the dangers. As any viewer of modern art knows, blatant pornography passes itself off as artistic expression, and arrogant amorality poses as openness and creativity. Art is very much about individualism, self-expression, and pushing the limits—regardless of who is offended in the process; Simon & Schuster once received a book proposal entitled *A Treasury of Filthy Religious Art Masterpieces*.[3]

I am *not* recommending that Christians casually and unquestioningly immerse themselves in the methods and mystique of the secular art world; I *am* suggesting that we acknowledge our fears and reevaluate what parts of the art world the Christian *can* be involved in, for the purpose of pursuing excellence and relevance—for the purpose of developing outstanding artists.

Step 2: We must learn the strategy of indirect communication.

C. S. Lewis wrote:

> The difficulty we are up against is this. We can make people (often) attend to the Christian point of view for half an hour or so; but the moment they have gone away from our lecture or laid down our article, they are plunged back into a world where the opposite position is taken for granted. As long as that situation exists, widespread success is simply impossible. . . . You can see this most easily if you look at it the other way round. Our Faith is not very likely to be shaken by any book on Hinduism. But if whenever we read an elementary book on Geology, Botany, Politics, or Astronomy, we found that its implications were Hindu, that would shake us. It is not the books written in direct defence of Materialism that make the modern man a materialist; it is the materialistic assumptions in all the other books.[4]

The problem, Lewis said, is that the enemy has sown so effectively that the non-Christian position is now taken for granted, and this prevailing atmosphere makes widespread belief in the gospel "simply impossible." This has not occurred through direct attacks on our faith, but through indirect communication—through thousands of communications about a myriad of topics, each subtly but powerfully assuming that the Christian worldview is unnecessary, outdated, or irrelevant. The solution? To countersow. "We must attack the enemy's line of communication," Lewis wrote. "What we want is not more little books about Christianity, but more little books by Christians on other subjects—with their Christianity latent."[5]

Lewis suggested that we begin to do exactly what our enemy has done to us, by learning the power of indirect communication. Instead of always attempting to persuade directly, we must learn to communicate on a thousand topics of interest to unbelievers with our Christianity "latent"—in such a way that the Christian worldview simply informs all of our other views. The net effect, if enough sowers pursued this strategy, could be to create a world where widespread *unbelief* would be "simply impossible." This cannot happen until Christians begin to understand the inherent power in indirect communication. The place to begin is by taking a closer look at the Bible itself. "Jesus was the master of indirection," Peterson said. "The parables are subversive. His hyperboles are indirect. There is a kind of outrageous quality to them that defies common sense, but later on the understanding comes."[6]

Step 3: We must grow in subtlety and patience.

Indirect communication requires great discipline on the part of a Christian. Having so much to say, how does she decide what to leave out? There is always the temptation to be more direct just to make sure they "get the message." This not a uniquely Christian temptation. It seems to be a struggle for anyone who has a message to get across, at least according to editor Ben Nyberg. In *The Best Writing on Writing,* he wrote about a common problem with "theme stories" he often receives, fiction stories where the author has a clear perspective to communicate.

> Ironically, it's usually when writers work too hard at making their intended statements clear and emphatic that they lose their grip on the dramatic illusion necessary to sustain their case. In their desire to spell things out so unambiguously no reader will mistake them, they may be tempted to thrust a more-or-less explicit story into the story's text, sometimes even putting wise words in the mouth of a "spokesman" character—whether he can speak them or not. The impression left may be earnest and intense, but it always has a hollow, unconvincing ring to it, because the writer has resorted to "special pleading" in support of a shaky argument.[7]

The rejection letter Nyberg includes with this kind of submission says: "Dear ____, If you really want to write tracts, maybe you ought to switch to propaganda's natural essay genre rather than trying to twist fiction to your ends."

It's no accident that I have referred to indirect communication as an art. Like all arts, it requires patience and discipline to learn. But learn it we must, or our communication will not appear indirect at all; it will simply look like propaganda. Philip Yancey writes in "Art and Propaganda" in *Open Windows:*

> The Christian public will applaud books in which every prayer is answered and every disease is healed; but to the degree those books do not reflect reality, they will become meaningless to a skeptical audience. Too often our evangelical literature appears to the larger world as strange and unconvincing as a Moonie tract or *Daily Worker* newspaper.[8]

Our indirect communication lacks power, Yancey says, because it isn't truly indirect. In our desire to make the message clear we sometimes violate the art we're attempting to use, and we end up simply writing propaganda.

There is one absolutely critical reason to talk about the need to develop our art. *Even if Christians are unconvinced of the value and power of art, the world will continue to use it.* The world, as we have noted earlier, is more than happy to sow, and it sows through art—through clever, subtle, gradual, indirect communication. "Today, as always," wrote Tony Campolo, "the greatest danger to those who would follow Jesus is not overt persecution by society, but subtle seduction by its values."[9] The greatest danger, he said, is not overt but subtle; not direct but indirect. While the world is successfully sowing and reaping a gradual harvest, the Christian world finds itself without the skills or even the desire to sow in return. This is the result:

- The greatest attacks on Christianity now come through art, not science.

- The most devastating blows to Christian belief are indirect, not frontal.

• The most damaging assaults on the Christian worldview are gradual, not immediate.

While the Christian world insists on short-term, confrontational proclamations to win its case, the world achieves its greatest victories through long-term, patient, persuasive appeals. The public school system has often been the focus of indoctrination for secular sowers, in areas from diversity training to environmentalism, from gay rights to safe sex, from evolution to the metric system. Cooperative teachers use colorful posters and role-play situations, and activist groups offer prizes to school children for the best essays written on their pet topic.

While we harvest, they sow; while we scorch, they water; while we measure the bounty of this generation, they prepare to gather the next.

Chapter 6 | OUTSIDE-IN

In 1939 a slender young correspondent for the *London Times* named Kim Philby was recruited to join the elite British intelligence agency, MI6. The Second World War was about to begin, and Philby was assigned to the sabotage and propaganda department. He excelled at his work, and soon he was promoted to counterespionage in foreign countries. By the end of the war, the British began to realize that the Soviet Union would pose the greatest postwar threat to British national security, and Philby was named to head the new department of Soviet counterintelligence. By 1949 he advanced yet again to become the British director of intelligence in Washington, D.C. Less than ten years into his remarkable career he was living in our nation's capital and serving as liaison between MI6 and our own CIA. He was a brilliant operative, a master of "the game" with access to the deepest secrets of two of the world's greatest superpowers. Philby was even being considered for the highest position in British intelligence: chief of MI6.

There was just one problem. Philby was a Soviet spy.

In intelligence lingo, a "mole" is an agent who is inserted into the political, military, or intelligence structure of a target nation with the specific objective of rising to a key position of influence and trust. At this point he is "switched on." He begins to betray high-level secrets to his home country, a country that he may not have seen for many years. At the time Philby was operative, no fewer than *five* Soviet moles had infiltrated the highest levels of Great Britain's intelligence community.

For a mole to be effective, he must possess three characteristics. First, *he must be a thorough part of the country he plans to infiltrate.* Fluency in the native language is not enough; he must know the jargon and the mannerisms as well. His knowledge of local customs and events, his family connections, even his hobbies and diversions all help to create an atmosphere of trust. "It couldn't be *him*—he's one of *us.*"

Second, *he must spend years rising to a level of influence.* A mole can't simply move to his target country and apply for a position of power and influence! He would be a foreigner, an outsider, never able to merit the complete trust of his colleagues. Similarly, he cannot rise to a position of influence without excelling at his work. He must work alongside his colleagues, rising through the ranks just as they must, being recognized and promoted because of his diligence and skill. With each patient step upward he increases his respect, his trust, his *opportunity.*

Third, *he must remember where his real allegiance lies.* A mole who becomes a complete part of his target country is no longer a mole at all—he's just another citizen. A good mole must live a double life; by all appearances his loyalties lie with his target country, but in his heart he remains fiercely devoted to his homeland. The ideal mole never forgets where he's from and what his mission is. "To betray," Kim Philby said near the end of his life, "one must first belong. I never belonged."[1]

We, too, can learn a lesson from the mole: *There is great potential for spiritual impact when a Christian becomes an insider by working his way to a key position of influence and trust.*

The Value of Being an Insider

In biblical history many triumphs were achieved or catastrophes averted through the crucial contribution of an insider. In the sixth century B.C., the city of Jerusalem was pillaged and plundered by the Babylonians, and more than sixty thousand of its inhabitants were carried away into exile. The city itself was left in ruins; the temple had been burned, and the defensive wall surrounding the city was leveled. The city lay in this desolate state for more than a century. The chief figure in reversing Jerusalem's fortunes was Nehemiah. Born during the exile, Nehemiah had patiently worked his way into a position of great honor and influence—cupbearer to the king of Persia. In ancient times, the cupbearer was a kind of valet; his chief job was to taste the wine served to the king as a precaution against poisoning by assassins. Obviously, this was a position of great trust. The cupbearer was close to those in authority and sometimes exercised considerable influence. It was because of his position as a trusted insider that Nehemiah was granted permission to return to Jerusalem to rebuild its wall and restore the people of God.

Just thirty years before Nehemiah made his request to rebuild the walls of Jerusalem, a different king was on the throne. This king, displeased with his current wife's rebellious attitude, decided to hold a talent search to find some new additions for his harem. One of the "winners" was Esther. "The king loved Esther more than all the women," the book of Esther tells us, "and she found favor and kindness with him more than all the virgins, so that he set the royal crown on her head and made her queen" (2:17). In a short period of time, Esther had risen to a level of tremendous influence. Soon she became aware of a plot to assassinate her husband; she exposed the plot and solidified the king's trust and gratitude. It was from this position as a trusted insider that Esther was able to deliver her people from an intended massacre by Haman, another high court official. Jewish people still celebrate this great deliverance with the Feast of Purim.

After Jesus' crucifixion, His body was requested by Joseph of Arimathea. Joseph was a wealthy man and a prominent member of the Sanhedrin, the seventy-one-member ruling council of Jerusalem. Joseph had become a follower of Jesus, but a secret one because of his fear of his colleagues. After Jesus' execution Joseph summoned the courage to go before Pilate and take responsibility for the burial. Pilate knew the risks involved and the rumors of a predicted resurrection. Would he have released the body to one of

Jesus' disciples, or to a member of Jesus' family, or even to a less respected member of the council? It was Joseph's status as a trusted insider that enabled him to bury the body of Jesus in a prominent,
secure location—a tomb cut into solid rock with a massive stone to
seal the opening. If Jesus had been buried in the flimsy, obscure tomb
of a poor man, how much more difficult would it have been to claim
that He rose from the dead?

Church history, too, contains lessons about the value of being
an insider. In 1780 William Wilberforce began a remarkable political
career by being elected to the House of Commons in England at the
tender age of twenty-one. Four years later, while traveling in France,
Wilberforce began to wrestle deeply with the conflict between his
political ambitions and the claims of Christ on his life. His agonized
soul-searching nearly drove him out of his mind. Finally, in despera-
tion, he sought the counsel of John Newton, the former slave trader
and now respected Christian. Newton advised Wilberforce to stay in
politics—to remain an insider in Parliament—because God just
might have elevated him to that position for a purpose. Indeed He
did. For the next twenty-two years Wilberforce tirelessly campaigned
for the abolition of the slave trade in Great Britain. Many others
were working to awaken the nation's conscience and to change popular sentiment toward slavery, but only an act of Parliament—only
those on the inside—could effect abolition. Through his exhaustive
efforts, the slave trade was abolished in 1807, and twenty-six years
later slavery itself was abolished in the entire British empire.

It's important to note that none of these individuals' greatest
contributions was in what we would consider "ministry." Rebuilding
the wall was a political action by Nehemiah; Esther's intercession was
a humanitarian effort; Joseph's request was a simple act of kindness
for a respected teacher; Wilberforce spent his entire career on social
justice. In each case, however, the "secular" activity had profound
spiritual implications. Each of these individuals was a great sower
who made possible the work of many harvesters who would follow.

It's always fascinating to play "It's a Wonderful Life" with historical figures. What if Nehemiah, Esther, Joseph, and William Wilberforce had never been born? What would have been the resulting
impact on history? If Nehemiah had never been born, the wall
around Jerusalem would certainly have been rebuilt, but probably

not for quite some time. Others had already tried and failed, halted by the resistance and slander of their enemies. Nehemiah's political clout allowed him to keep the favor of the king even in the face of false accusation. Attempting to rebuild the wall *without* the Persian king's express permission would have been viewed as an act of aggression and would have been suppressed with force. The wall would have been *eventually* rebuilt—but when?

If Esther had never been born, the massacre of the Jews under Haman would almost certainly have taken place, with far-reaching historical consequences. The massacre could have included both Nehemiah and Ezra!

If Joseph of Arimathea had not been there to claim the body of Jesus, the body would still have been buried—though it would certainly not have been released to anyone openly sympathetic to Jesus' cause. Perhaps another secret follower like Nicodemus would have risen to the occasion. If not, the body would have been disposed of by the Roman officials. In this scenario, what would the account of the Resurrection have looked like?

If William Wilberforce had never been born, the slave trade would still have been abolished in Great Britain, but not until much later. It's difficult to overestimate the role this one man played in ending British slavery. It was as though Wilberforce had been specifically created to take on this one monumental task: He was a passionate Christian, a tireless politician, a brilliant orator, and even an old college chum of the prime minister! If he had not been born, who else could have combined the vast array of skills and fearless convictions necessary to see this task through? And without the end of slavery in Great Britain, what would have provided the impetus for abolishing slavery here in the United States?

Calling Insiders Out

What if Nehemiah, Esther, Joseph, and Wilberforce *had* been born, but lacked their status as insiders? What if Nehemiah had been just another scribe, or Esther just another girl in the harem, or Joseph of Arimathea a simple Jewish merchant? What if William Wilberforce had been the passionate Christian that he was—but no *more* than that? Suppose John Newton's counsel to him had been, "It's obvious that

God is calling you into the ministry, and if God calls you to follow Him, don't stoop to be a king or a member of Parliament." Would his convictions *alone* have allowed him to have the same impact?

What if Wilberforce were alive today, and in his agonized searching he sought the counsel of a modern-day pastor or Christian leader? How many would counsel Wilberforce to stay in politics? How many would encourage a perfectly good candidate for full-time ministry to remain instead in a secular vocation for the possibility of having some uncertain, nebulous future impact?

How many would encourage him to *sow* instead of *harvest*?

The answer, I think, is very few. Despite the lessons exemplified in Scripture and church history, most Christians are unconvinced of the value of sowing and suspicious of any "calling" to be an insider. Instead, Christians exhort sowers to grow in their commitment by joining the harvest, and they admonish insiders to come out and make a difference. I call this approach to the Christian life "outside-in."

According to the outside-in philosophy, the greatest sign of a Christian's maturity and commitment is his willingness to *go*—most anywhere will do. The organization of Campus Crusade for Christ, of which I am a part, has more than six thousand staff members serving in various capacities in the United States. In every technical sense of the word we are missionaries—yet virtually every one of our staff has at one time or another been asked, "How can you be a missionary if you work in the United States?" In other words: How can you be a real missionary unless you *go?* In our organization we have a tongue-in-cheek definition of a missionary: "Someone who has crossed a large body of water."

This is much more than a confusion about what it means to be a true missionary. Deeply embedded in the evangelical culture is the mind-set that real ministry always involves (1) leaving what you do now and (2) going somewhere else. A sermon by a visiting overseas missionary challenged us with the thought that "Two-thirds of GOD is GO." I must confess that the first thought that crossed my mind was, *Two-thirds of GOD is OD, too. What does that prove?*

The Outside-In Philosophy

Consider the outside-in philosophy in practice. John is a senior vice president at a large advertising agency. He has worked his way up the corporate ladder for several years and now holds an executive level position in his agency. John has also been a Christian for several years now, and he has experienced a growing desire to make an impact for Christ. He has been involved in a few Bible studies and local outreaches and he enjoyed the experiences very much. He would love to do more, but how? When? Like William Wilberforce, sometimes he agonizes over what he should do. Does he attempt to have some spiritual impact through the vocation he feels strongly attracted to, or does he move instead toward full-time ministry—*real* ministry? Does he *stay* or *go?*

The outside-in philosophy concludes that John should go. "Think of how John spends his average day," the outside-inner reasons. "Think of how much of his time is spent on expense reports, employee performance reviews, budget projections. . . . Imagine the impact he could have if he could devote his full time to ministry! Imagine the difference he could make if he could free himself from the distractions of all the daily monotony! What would a really *committed* Christian do? He would lay down his life. He would take up his cross. He would *go.*"

And then, as strange as it may sound, John would be encouraged to go back. "The point of *going*," the outside-inner explains, "isn't simply to *leave.* The point of going is to give John the chance to lay aside all distractions and entanglements to devote his full attention to becoming trained and equipped for ministry. Then, when he's ready, he can go back in and make a *real* difference. After all, who knows more about the needs of advertising people than an ex-advertising executive?" Thus outside-inners often encourage ex-businessmen to work with executives, ex-convicts to work in prisons, college alumni to work with college students, and ex-politicians to work with legislators. Now that John is committed, now that he has gone, *now* he can have an impact.

Unfortunately, this is often where John's impact ends.

Imagine John, now fully trained and equipped, arriving at the front door of his old ad agency, ready to "make a difference." Where does he begin? He begins by calling on old acquaintances and reestablishing old contacts. He finds that some are still there, but others have retired or have been transferred. Soon those contacts are exhausted, but John wants to gain deeper access to the agency. He wants to meet more people, people from other departments, people he has never met. But how? He can no longer simply wander the halls and knock on office doors or hang out by the water cooler. He has to look for someone on the *inside,* someone who believes in what he's doing, someone who can introduce him to others.

He has to look for someone *exactly like the person he used to be.*

The outside-in approach to the Christian life could be summarized this way: Every true calling from God is a calling *out.* To remain inside is to give up the chance to make a *real* difference, and it may reveal a simple lack of true commitment. Once you are outside you can be trained and consecrated to go back in and conduct real, valuable ministry.

The Washington-based Christian Embassy is a ministry that serves men and women in the highest spheres of influence: the federal government, the Pentagon, and the diplomatic community. Washington is an extremely fast-paced, intense community, and those who work there tend to have a closed-door policy. No one simply "drops by" unannounced. Meetings take place by appointment only and are scheduled in fifteen-minute increments. Several levels of administrative staff protect those in positions of the greatest power and influence, like members of Congress. Call and ask to speak to your senator. You'll be greeted by a friendly voice—that of a college intern. From there you'll get an administrative secretary, then a staff member, maybe eventually the chief of staff. It would take a minor miracle, however, to get through to the senator himself.

Yet the Christian Embassy has regularly conducted ministry with members of Congress. How is this possible? At the beginning of a session of Congress, the Embassy may have only a single contact with a member—an insider. That member, who attends a brief weekly Bible study in the Capitol, may agree to host a luncheon for freshman representatives at which the Embassy is introduced. Or the member may arrange a private introduction between an Embassy staff member and one of his colleagues. It is a highly relational, high-risk, incremental form of ministry—and a lot of work can be undone in a short period of time. Members must constantly bid for reelection. In a single bad election season the Embassy can lose the majority of its sympathetic insiders, and the ministry must virtually start over. Those who are outsiders depend completely on insiders for ministry to take place.

Though the Christian Embassy is a unique kind of ministry, it faces the same dilemma as many others who take an outside-in approach to ministry. We teach people that to have a real ministry they must go, but the moment they leave they become dependent on others who stayed. We pray for people to go, then we hope to find people who didn't. We begin to look like flies on a windowpane: those on the inside want out, and those on the outside want in.

Strengths of Outside-In

I don't mean to create the impression that the outside-in philosophy is completely mistaken. In fact, it's based on some very good observations about the real world. For many Christians, the frantic pace of daily life will *forever* prevent them from gaining the knowledge and training they need to have an impact on others. How else are they to clear their schedules and find the time unless they in some sense *go?* And what about the reality of competing time demands? How much time can an insider spend during office hours doing ministry with others? Is John paid to be a minister or a vice president? An outsider, on the other hand, is free to use his time as he chooses. There is a difficult trade-off to be considered here: the value of time and focus versus the value of being an insider. It's not an easy choice to make. What's the good of being an insider if you lack the knowledge or experience to take advantage of your status? But what's the good of going if, by becoming an outsider, you lose influence and access to the very people you want to reach?

From the outside-in perspective, there are two options: (1) you can come out and be trained to harvest, possibly losing valuable influence you once possessed, or (2) you can remain inside and attempt to harvest, muddling by the best you can with competing time demands and no training. You can harvest as an *insider* or you can harvest as an *outsider.*

But there is a third option, an option that has tremendous value —though few Christians currently recognize it as true ministry at all. It is the philosophy of inside-out, in which insiders are encouraged to stay where they are—and to *sow.*

An Inside Job

Sowing is an inside job. The sower understands that his position as an insider does indeed grant him access to people and opportunities to harvest, and when the fruit is ripe it's always time to pick. But the sower recognizes that his insider status grants him many other opportunities aside from direct evangelism that are also of great value—perhaps not today or tomorrow, but in the future. They are opportunities to sow: to water, to cultivate the soil, to prepare for a future harvest. As we said before, neither Nehemiah, Esther, Joseph of Arimathea, nor William Wilberforce were involved in what we would today consider "ministry," though no one could doubt the tremendous impact of their efforts to sow. What does sowing look like today, and what can the modern sower do to have that kind of impact? In chapter 12 we'll look at a variety of specific sowing activities in the marketplace. Each requires patience, perspective, and a long-term view of ministry; each has tremendous potential for eventual impact; and each requires an *insider*.

Christians are wary of the inside-out approach to ministry for two reasons. First, as we said before, a mole who blends in *too* well is no longer a mole at all—he's just another citizen. To be honest, a Christian who attempts to become an insider sometimes finds that the process requires virtually *all* of his time and attention. It's a difficult thing to live a double life: to invest the time and energy necessary to earn influence and trust, all the while remembering the interests of the homeland. Not all insiders turn out to be a William Wilberforce. A lot of them just seem to disappear into the culture. We watch for years as an insider grows into a position of trust and influence, waiting for that moment when he makes some critical contribution, only to find that the moment never comes. What was the value of that? The outsider, even if he has lost the benefits of being on the inside, at least maintains a clear sense of purpose and identity. He knows who he is and he knows what he is supposed to do —even if he has trouble doing it.

The second reason Christians are wary of the inside-out approach goes much deeper. To remain an insider seems to suggest apathy or concession. A recent Christian book warns on the cover: *We want it both ways. We want the excitement of a secular culture, but we want the benefits of the Christian faith. Thus we make . . . The Great Compromise.* Isn't that exactly what the insider seems to do? What is her *real* motive for remaining on the inside? What is she afraid to give up? She talks about her desire to make a difference; why doesn't she just *go?*

Deeply imbedded in our insistence on *going* is a kind of separatism. "'Therefore, come out from their midst and be separate,' says the Lord," Paul wrote, paraphrasing Isaiah. "'And do not touch what is unclean; and I will welcome you'" (2 Corinthians 6:17). Paul's warning was to prevent us from forming intimate relationships with those who don't hold our value system and priorities—from being "unequally yoked" with unbelievers. But evangelicals sometimes expand Paul's words, as though he was warning us away from all contact with the unbelieving world. Some Christians begin to assume that sanctification itself is an ever-increasing process of coming out, being separate, and touching no unclean thing. The result is an attitude of separatism that has encouraged a polarization between the Christian and non-Christian worlds. Our culture seems to want nothing to do with the Christian world, and that's OK with us. There is no doubt that our two worlds are racing rapidly away from each other. I wonder sometimes, who is moving faster?

The insider, however, requires intimate, ongoing contact with the unbelieving world—a contact that our separatist mind-set has no stomach for. Just as we reserve our greatest admiration for those who leave everything and go, we reserve our strongest suspicions for those who remain and yet claim to be somehow committed to Christ. Sowers make us nervous; they seem to represent some kind of carnality or dalliance with the world. We look at the sower among us and ask suspiciously, "Whose side is he *on,* anyway?" Because we want to know clearly who is for us and who is against us, we like to have the sowers stand up and testify from time to time—*even if the exposure compromises the sower's effectiveness as an insider.*

Imagine the director of an intelligence agency who becomes suspicious about the true allegiance of his moles in foreign countries, so he asks for a public show of hands: "Who's on our side?" The moles obediently raise their hands. The director walks away smug and satisfied, but the moles have a different feeling entirely. They have been compromised. They have been forced to surrender their status as insiders—a status that may have taken years to obtain. Statistics show that moles who have been exposed are much more prone to unfortunate accidents, like automobiles that explode without warning.

As silly as this scenario sounds, this is exactly what we Christians often do with those who want to practice an inside-out form of ministry. A musician who is rumored to be a Christian wins a Grammy Award. As we watch the awards presentation, televised to millions, our most fervent hope is that she'll testify, very much as the gay community hopes that someone on their side will come out of the closet. We hope that, in her acceptance speech, she'll look toward heaven and dedicate her award to the Lord Jesus Christ and perhaps throw in a few words of exhortation for the viewing audience. I guess *that* will prove whose side she's on. If she fails to do this, we doubt her maturity or true commitment; we may even feel a little betrayed. In a society made up of a thousand special-interest groups, it's a powerful thing to be able to say of a famous celebrity, "She's on our side!"

But how powerful *is* it—compared to the power of a musician, with the full respect of her colleagues, recording outstanding music that undergirds a Christian worldview? Is her brief testimony really a powerful form of persuasion to the viewers, or is it more of a powerful form of self-satisfaction for us? What if, when she testifies publicly as to her true loyalties and religious views, a producer in the audience decides he would rather not work with her in the future? What if her record company considers her testimony a little embarrassing and decides to pull back a little on her promotion for the next few months? What is the *relative* good done by her testimony? This is not an easy question, but it's a question that every sower must struggle with—and have the courage to answer for herself.

As I said before, the dilemma becomes greater if we think only in terms of harvesting. It's easy to understand the value of straightforward gospel music—the music of the harvester. It's also easy to understand the value of attempting to market that same kind of music to non-Christians—if that's possible. The value of both is obvious; after all, they're both attempts to harvest. What's *not* as easy for most evangelicals to understand is the value of the music of the sower.

A sower's music might take many forms, but it would always

possess two qualities. First, it would refuse to exalt or endorse any value that undermines a biblical worldview. A sower's music would not, for example, lament the ultimate meaninglessness of life or extol the pleasures of casual sex. Second, a sower's music, in form and content, would seek to undergird and strengthen a biblical view of life. It might praise the seeker of truth, or reflect on the beauty and design inherent in nature, or do any one of a thousand other things that are consistent with a biblical image of the world. On first hearing, it might seem to say little or nothing at all about God—directly.

"But that's not *Christian* music," some would complain. No, not if by Christian music you mean straightforward gospel music, music that attempts to harvest. This is music, as C. S. Lewis would say, with the Christianity *latent*. It's an *indirect* communication that has tremendous potential for influence—over time. Imagine, as Lewis would say, if every time a teenager turned on a radio, the music he heard was not proclaiming a Christian message, but was simply consistent with a biblical worldview. Would that be of any value? Would it have any effect on the mind-set of the teenager over time? And could it have any effect on the way that teenager might one day respond to the direct appeal of a harvester?

Sometimes the director of the intelligence agency *doesn't* call for a show of hands. Instead, he begins to call his moles home—perhaps to help train others in the art of being a good mole. But if Kim Philby had been regularly invited home to visit the Soviet Union, wouldn't that have reduced his effectiveness? This is what often happens in the case of our own insiders. Imagine that the fictional John had chosen to remain as an insider to sow within his advertising agency, and that he had experienced remarkable success. Soon John is contacted by a large church in his area that shares an interest in making inroads into the business community. Could John come and spend a few hours speaking to them about his strategy? Could he spend a few weeks helping equip others to do what he has done? Could he spend a few years directing a new ministry designed to reproduce his efforts on a national scale?

If he does, John would have unknowingly begun what I call the "outward spiral." He began as a true insider, one of a rare breed of Christians who actually has intimate contact with unbelievers. He begins to advise other Christians, then to train them, then to lead them. More and more of his time is spent with Christians instead of unbelievers. By the time the outward spiral is complete, John is no longer an insider at all. His many visits to the homeland have begun to occupy his full time and attention. He has become an outsider, residing completely in the Christian world.

A word of caution is appropriate here: My metaphor of the "mole" has its limits. Our moles have been told by their Master not to forsake assembling with other believers. In fact, if John desires to be a truly effective insider, he will need the encouragement and support of other believers more than ever! I am not recommending that we simply abandon Christians deep within strategic areas of the secular world, hoping that their faith and motivation somehow survive the experience. As I'll argue in chapter 13, a sower needs ongoing interaction with other believers—especially other sowers in similar fields—precisely because he is attempting to operate in foreign and potentially hostile territory.

When I caution against the Christian community's temptation to "invite our moles home," I have two specific concerns in mind: first, that we are so concerned that Christians make clear that "they're on our side" that we encourage statements of faith in their place of ministry, sometimes reducing the Christian's potential to have subtle, gradual, ongoing influence. My second concern is that outward spiral; we not only seek to maintain fellowship with our moles, we urge them toward an ever-increasing commitment of time, energy, and focus on the Christian world. This regularly happens to the best of our insiders. We seem to find it difficult to leave them alone and simply let them do what they do without asking for a show of hands or inviting them home. We find it even more difficult to recognize sowing as a valuable form of ministry, and to help and encourage them in any way we can. Could that be why so little sowing takes place? And could that be one of the reasons we now find ourselves talking about the Last Harvest?

No sooner had Kim Philby taken up residence in Washington than he learned one of America's biggest secrets. Code-named VENONA, it was a code-breaking operation attempting to decipher a huge backlog of intercepted Soviet communications. As each message was slowly decoded, it became alarmingly clear that the Soviets had successfully placed *hundreds* of agents in Great Britain and the United States. Philby watched nervously as friend after friend was betrayed—and as clue after clue began to raise suspicions about Philby himself. One winter evening Philby slipped out of a dinner party unnoticed and disappeared from the face of the earth. Six weeks later, Moscow announced that the Soviet Union had granted him political asylum. The greatest mole in history had been called home.

Philby became a kind of national hero as the greatest intelligence agent in Soviet history. He was given the honorary title of full general in the KGB and was provided a large apartment and a generous pension. He was even granted the Order of Lenin, the Soviet Union's highest decoration. But Philby was not a happy man. He had expected to continue his stellar career, to be appointed to some influential position within the KGB, perhaps to direct British intelligence—only this time from Soviet soil. It was not to be. Philby's entire usefulness was as a *mole,* and once he was no longer an insider he lost all value to his homeland. He was granted a titular position and served only as an honored guest at endless government dinner parties. Philby died a disillusioned alcoholic, a frustrated British exile, a man with no purpose. As an insider, he was the greatest secret agent in Soviet history. As an outsider, he was just another citizen.

Chapter 7 | INNOCENTS ABROAD

"A man was going down from Jerusalem to Jericho," Jesus began. "He fell among robbers, and they stripped him and beat him, and went away, leaving him half dead."

The story begins. A naked figure lay beaten and unconscious in the middle of a road. Was he Jew? Gentile? Young? Old? We aren't told. He was any man—every man.

Hours passed before another traveler approached—a priest.

The priest stopped in astonishment. *Is he dead? How long has he been here? How did this happen?* He glanced nervously at the surrounding hillsides. *Is it safe for me to be here?* His first instinct was to rush to the man, to lift his head, to look for signs of life.

The priest took two quick steps forward, then stopped abruptly. Beneath the man's left ear lay a crimson pool.

Blood. A bodily discharge. Today I must serve in the temple. If I touch this discharge, the Law says I am unclean and cannot serve in the temple. Seven days for ceremonial cleansing! And what will the elders think of me when I declare myself "unclean"?

The priest slowly began to circle the broken body . . .

I think he is dead. Yes, I am certain he is dead. To touch a dead body is a month of uncleanness. What can I do for him if he is already in Abraham's bosom? Let the dead bury their own dead.

And so, after saying a prayer for God's mercy and kindness, the priest walked quickly away.

Later that day, a Levite came around the bend. He almost stumbled over the motionless form before jumping back in shock and disgust. Like the priest, his first instinct was to rush forward, to touch, to help. Like the priest, he resisted the instinct.

Who is this man? What family is he from? The Levite poked at the body with the tip of his sandal. No response.

Why does no one come to his aid? Does no one care about this man? What has he done to deserve this fate?

The last question lingered in his mind . . .

The Law tells us, "He does not leave the guilty unpunished; he punishes the children and their children for the sin of the fathers to the third and fourth generation."[1] *Does not the Lord prosper and prolong the days of the righteous? Surely this man is under the judgment of God!*

As the Levite studied the silent figure, the man's face seemed to change. Moments before, it had been the face of an innocent victim. Now it was the face of a sinner, a hardened transgressor, perhaps even a murderer.

"The Righteous One takes note of the house of the wicked and brings the wicked to ruin."[2] *Who am I to turn back the hand of the Lord? I must not enter into this man's sin.*

And so, saying a prayer of thanksgiving for God's protection, the Levite continued on his way.

As he walked, a fellow traveler approached. Though the road was narrow, their eyes never met. As they passed, a curse swelled in the Levite's mind, an ethnic slur that belongs to every culture and time and has taken a thousand different forms. In the Levite's mind, it took the form *Samaritan!*

The Samaritan's Jewish ancestors had lived near Judea for more than a millennium. Seven centuries before, Assyria besieged ancient Israel and carried off much of the Jewish population into exile. The land was repopulated with conquered peoples from all over the Near East. Over time, the Jewish remnant of Samaria intermarried with the foreigners. The resulting Samaritans were a loathsome symbol of compromise and unfaithfulness to the Jews. *Half-breed . . . collaborator . . . idolater . . . Samaritan!*

The Samaritan traveler halted at the broken and bloody figure before him. Kneeling by his side, he reached out to brush back the man's tangled hair from his face. He stopped abruptly; taking the flask from around his neck, he first washed the dust from his own hands before touching the figure before him. As he tended to the man's wounds, the Samaritan, like the Levite, noticed that the man's face seemed to change. Moments before he had looked like an anonymous stranger. Now, as the Samaritan looked upon the stranger's battered face, he saw a friend, a neighbor—he saw *himself.*

I hope he does not awaken. He might take offense at being touched by a Samaritan. I do not wish to make him unclean.

The Samaritan lifted the man and carried him to his donkey. He took him to an inn, where he cared for him at his own expense.[3]

The tale had come to an end. All that remained to be told was the moral of the story. Jesus said to the lawyer, "Which of these three do you think was a neighbor to the man who fell into the hands of robbers?"

"The Sam . . . the Samar . . ." the lawyer stammered. He couldn't even say the word. "The one who had mercy on him."

"Go and do likewise." Act more like a Samaritan, and you'll be a better Jew.

The parable of the Good Samaritan is one of the best-known stories in Western literature. Like all great stories, it operates on a number of levels. It's like an onion; as each layer of truth is removed, another layer is revealed. On the surface, it's a story about what it means to love your neighbor. On a deeper level, it's a story about racism and prejudice. Near its core, it's a story about separatism and pride.

The Bible contains hundreds of stories and parables, some of which are hard to understand. The Good Samaritan is easy. There are good guys to applaud and bad guys to boo and hiss. I'm amazed how much I resemble the Samaritan; I shake my head in disbelief at the blatant selfishness of the priest and Levite. If I remove only the first layer of the story, I walk away vindicated and self-satisfied. But if I dig deeper, the story suddenly turns on me. All at once, I realize what Jesus really meant . . .

I am the priest and Levite. And so are *you.*

Maintaining Purity in the Midst of Corruption

William Bennett included the parable of the Good Samaritan in his *Book of Virtues.* In his introduction to the parable, Bennett wrote, "The traveler who comes to the wounded man's aid here is the least likely to show sympathy."[4] On the contrary. I think Jesus knew that the Samaritan was *more* likely to show compassion, for one simple reason: He was the only one who could *afford* to.

He was already unclean.

The ironic thing about the parable of the Good Samaritan is that, even though the story contains two obvious bad guys, neither of them is a *complete* bad guy. What prevented the priest and Levite from stopping to help the wounded man? In each case it was probably a fear of defilement, the risk of ceremonial uncleanness. Their concept of uncleanness wasn't just some silly imagination—it was derived from Old Testament Law. To some extent, their choice to ignore the wounded man was a choice to obey the Law and to please God.

To *some* extent, Jesus posed the priest and Levite with a moral dilemma—they had to choose between competing biblical demands. Is it more important to strictly adhere to the ceremonial laws or to help a fellow human being made in the image of God? Their choice in this matter would reveal a lot about their true understanding of the Law—and even more about the condition of their hearts. When Jesus was reproached for healing a man on the Sabbath, He became angry. He expected His critics to know better. Faced with their own moral dilemma, they had failed to choose wisely and compassionately. Their poor priorities revealed a lot about them, and Jesus was "grieved at their hardness of heart" (Mark 3:5).

Jesus could have made the parable of the Good Samaritan much simpler. A priest, a Levite, and a Samaritan were told of a poor man who needed money. Would they contribute? The wealthy priest and Levite said no; the poor Samaritan said yes—end of story. Evil bad guys, a compassionate good guy, and an unmistakable choice. The story would have been much simpler—and much more boring. Jesus chose to give His parable a quality that all great dramatic stories possess: *It captures the complexity of choices we all have to make in the real world.*

Biblical Principles in Tension

Life commonly faces us with moral dilemmas, and Christians often feel the tension of competing biblical demands. Sometimes the entire Christian life appears to be a series of tensions or balances that each of us must maintain, both in belief and practice. God is all-loving and at the same time all-just. God is completely sovereign, but in some sense we each possess free will. God is omnipresent, but all the fullness of deity dwelt in Jesus in bodily form. No one can fully explain these paradoxes; they are all true beliefs that the Christian must hold in balance in his mind.

Practice is no easier than belief. I'm supposed to be *in* the world, but not *of* the world. How exactly do I do both at the same time? I'm supposed to give to Caesar what is Caesar's, and to God what is God's. That's easy to apply when you have to pay taxes, but not when you've been drafted to go to Vietnam.

All acts of balancing, whether physical or mental, are inherently exhausting. Walking down a sidewalk is almost effortless, but walking precisely down a straight line painted on the sidewalk is tiring. A three-minute routine on a balance beam can exhaust an Olympic athlete. Imagine walking a tightrope strung between the towers of the World Trade Center! As the cost of failure increases, so do the tension and fatigue.

Because maintaining balance is so tiring, most people who find themselves on a tightrope instinctively look for the best direction to fall. Better to be at rest in error than to have to maintain the wearisome balance of truth. This has been the source of much of the heresy in the history of the church. How can Jesus be fully God and fully man? I don't know, so I'll just choose which way to fall: He's God or He's man. How can God be sovereign if at the same time man possesses free will? I can't reconcile the two, so I become a hyper-Calvinist or an Arminian. I may be mistaken, but at least I'm off the tightrope.

Falling Off the Tightrope

Christians today seem to almost universally neglect one biblical tension. Jesus described it when He gave instructions to His disciples before sending them out on their own. "Behold," he warned them, "I send you out as sheep in the midst of wolves; so be shrewd as serpents and innocent as doves" (Matthew 10:16).

In our dealings with unbelievers, Jesus said, we are to be both *shrewd* and *innocent*. One commentator described the tension this way: "His followers were to be, not prudent toward outsiders and innocent toward God, but both prudent and innocent in their mission to outsiders. . . . The balance is difficult, but not a little of Jesus' teaching combines such poles of meaning."[5]

The strange thing about *this* tightrope is that evangelicals almost without exception choose to fall off to the same side, as though the other side doesn't even exist. What a peculiar anomaly! The law of averages tells us that roughly half should err to each side, yet some strange suction draws us all irresistibly toward *innocence* and away from *shrewdness*.

The word translated "shrewd" is the Greek word *phronimos*, which means "prudent, sensible, or practically wise." Why should we neglect such useful qualities? Perhaps the problem is with the metaphor "shrewd *as serpents*." The last shrewd serpent we bumped into, in the Garden of Eden, caused a great deal of trouble. The result was a loss of innocence. Surely the pursuit of shrewdness can only lead to a further loss of innocence. The very word *shrewd* seems to suggest some form of carnality; it has the connotation of slyness or deception.

We've all heard countless admonitions to pursue personal purity and innocence; when was the last time you heard a sermon entitled "Pursuing Personal Shrewdness"? We remember that Paul wrote, "Do all things without grumbling or disputing; so that you will prove yourselves to be blameless and innocent . . ." (Philippians 2:14–15a). Why do we overlook the fact that he also wrote, "I want you to be wise in what is good and innocent in what is evil" (Romans 16:19b)?

Shrewdness without innocence easily degenerates into cheap craftiness or cunning—but innocence without shrewdness becomes ignorance, foolishness, and naiveté.

It's important to take note of the *timing* of Jesus' warning to His disciples. The disciples had watched Jesus teach the multitudes, heal the sick, cast out demons, and even walk on water without any mention of their need for shrewdness. The disciples had worked, traveled, prayed, and fasted together without any special need for prudence or practical wisdom. *It was not until they were sent out to have personal contact with unbelievers that they were warned of the need to be both innocent and wise.*

Because of our allergic reaction to shrewdness, Christians today often appear ignorant and insensitive in our dealings with the non-Christian world. As long as we remain within the fellowship of the saints our foolishness and naiveté will be forgiven. But step outside the camp, and it's a cold, cruel world out there.

Nothing but the Truth

In March of 1997, Green Bay Packer defensive lineman and ordained minister Reggie White was invited to speak before the Wisconsin state legislature. As a part of his prepared presentation he spoke of how God had given various ethnic groups different gifts. "Black people are very gifted in what we call worship and celebration," he said. "A lot of us like to dance. And if you go to a black church, you'll see people jumping up and down." Of Hispanics, he said: "Hispanics were gifted in family structure. And you can see a Hispanic person, and they could put twenty or thirty people in one home." As for whites: "You guys know how to tap into money." Then he spoke about homosexuals: "Homosexuality is a decision. It's not a race. People from all different ethnic backgrounds are living this lifestyle. But people from all different ethnic backgrounds also are liars and cheaters and malicious and backstabbing."

Legislators were shocked at what appeared to be offensive stereotyping of ethnic groups. Gay rights groups immediately demanded that White's sponsors, including Nike and Campbell's Soup, cancel his endorsement contracts. CBS Sports, which was about to offer White a broadcasting job, withdrew the contract offer.

In his first interview after the event, with Peggy Wehmeyer of ABC News, White expressed surprise at the angry response to what he considered harmless, inoffensive comments. "If you go to Japan or any Asian country," he had said in his speech, "they can turn a television into a watch." Asked about his remark, he replied, "Is that true or not?" In fact, White's perspective on *all* of his comments seemed to reduce to one point: He had spoken the truth, and that was all that was required of him. "I'm going to speak the truth," he said regarding his comments about homosexuals, "and I'm going to speak against those things that's hurting our children, that's killing off my people. And if people think that's a contradiction and that's hate, then they need to take that to God, take that up with God and not Reggie White." Wehmeyer asked if the loss of his broadcasting contract with CBS made him angry: "That don't make me mad. I'm angry because what I said was the truth."[6]

Not long after the Reggie White incident, I sat in a church listening to a sermon by the president of a northeastern Bible college. He made reference to Reggie White's speech before the Wisconsin legislature and the resultant backlash. "What drew the ire of the legislators and the media elite alike," he claimed, "was Reggie's bold application of the word 'sin' to homosexuality." In fact, it was a little more than that; it was also the implied connection with the words "liar," "cheater," "backstabber," and "malicious."

The picture that emerged from the Bible college president's sermon was that Reggie White had courageously spoken the truth and was now being victimized for it. He was presented as a kind of mini-martyr, someone to be admired and even emulated. I disagree. No one can deny that Reggie White was courageous or that he had said what he believed to be true. No one can deny that he was innocent— *but he was not shrewd.*

"Like Reggie White," the Bible college president proclaimed, "you and I as Christians are facing the challenge of living Christianly in today's culture." Indeed it is a challenge—but living Christianly is more than the challenge of being courageous and telling the truth. It's *equally* the challenge of being "prudent, sensible, and practically wise," especially in our dealings with unbelievers. White's comments might have gone unnoticed within the walls of an evangelical church, but he was no longer *in* an evangelical church. Shrewdness should have led him to adjust his comments, and especially his vocabulary, to the mind-set of his secular listeners.

"I'm not politically correct," White said unapologetically. "Man wrote up the politically correct laws. God didn't." Yes, but it was the apostle Paul and not the Political Correctness Movement that told us to "Respect what is right in the sight of all men" (Romans 12:17). In conservative circles it has become a popular act of defiance to be "politically incorrect." Sometimes, "I'm politically incorrect" is just another way of saying, "I'm completely ignorant of the values and attitudes of the people I hope to persuade." The most common complaint about political correctness is that it's tiresome. Do I really have to *bother* with all that? Why can't I just say it *my* way? You can, if your goal is simple proclamation and not persuasion. Political correctness *is* tiresome. So are all attempts to understand the values and attitudes of another person. So are all attempts to be shrewd. It may be no more than simple laziness that prevents many innocents from pursuing the critical counterbalance of *wisdom*.

Building a Secure House

The book of Proverbs recommends three objects of desire that are more worth obtaining than gold or jewels: knowledge, understanding, and wisdom. Knowledge is simple information: names, dates, facts, and statistics. Understanding is the ability to sort out this information, to give it some kind of priority, and to comprehend its true meaning. Wisdom, which we are advised to seek above all, is the ability to apply knowledge skillfully to real-life situations.

Proverbs 24:3-4 tells us, "By wisdom a house is built, and by understanding it is established; and by knowledge the rooms are filled with all precious and pleasant riches." Notice the construction schedule for this house. The main structure of the house is accomplished through wisdom; the structure is made solid and secure through understanding; finally, it's decorated with knowledge. It's strange that modern builders have reversed this building code entirely. As we noted in chapter 4, our almost limitless technological ability to gather, store, and disseminate data has led us to become enamored with information *alone*—and Christians take part in this obsession. Modern Christian houses are built from sheer masses of information; we do our best to make the structure secure by comprehending what we can of this mountain of data; finally, some time after the move-in date, we decorate with a smattering of wisdom. The result of our modern construction techniques is that *Christians often lack wisdom—the ability to apply their biblical knowledge to real-life situations.*

In 1983 I created the Communication Center, a kind of training center designed to teach Christians to be more creative, confident, accurate, relevant, and skillful communicators of biblical truth—specifically to unbelievers. Our original training program was six weeks long and was attended by both college students and professional Christian workers. Each student was assigned a trainer who worked closely with the student as he prepared his two required presentations. The process began with the student analyzing his intended audience and then selecting an appropriate topic, which had to be approved by his trainer. That first student-trainer interaction often sounded like this:

> TRAINER: OK, who is your intended audience?
> STUDENT: Male college students living in the SAE fraternity house at the University of Iowa.
> TRAINER: And what have you selected as an appropriate topic?
> STUDENT: I want to speak about "Sex."
> TRAINER: OK. Let's begin by asking, "What does the Bible have to say about sex?"
> STUDENT: *(The student pauses here, as though this might be a trick question.)* It's wrong.
> TRAINER: Is that what you're going to say in front of the SAE house? "Good evening. Sex: It's wrong"? Let me put it another way: What does the Bible have to say to an SAE who asks, "What in the world is wrong with having responsible, protected sex with my girlfriend whom I will probably marry?"
> STUDENT: *(Long pause)* I'm also thinking about speaking on "Prophecy."

What I discovered after several years of this kind of interaction is that, because of the separatism that exists in the evangelical world, Christians tend to learn the Bible as an isolated topic. They understand biblical doctrine, but not what it has to do with business or politics or the family. They understand biblical morality, but not how to apply it to the complexity of modern relationships. They are superbly prepared to answer questions that non-Christians quit asking two generations ago.

John Wesley once commented that a mature Christian should be able to put his finger down anywhere in the Bible and work from that point to the gospel. That's an admirable goal, but I would like to suggest another skill that's needed just as much because of those modern construction techniques: A mature Christian should be able to put his finger down anywhere in *today's newspaper* and work from *that* point to the gospel. Christians today must stop being satisfied with randomly collected biblical data and begin to aggressively pursue *wisdom*—the ability to apply what they know to their own lives and to the lives of unbelievers around them.

Christians need to remember that we have been instructed by our Master to maintain a balance between innocence *and* shrewdness. Obedience lies in achieving the balance, not in committing the lesser of evils. No one will ever be able to stand before God and say proudly, "I failed at the balance between innocence and shrewdness, but at least I erred toward innocence." To fall off the tightrope to *either* side is an *equal* blunder. In the Last Harvest, with our heightened emphasis on courage and our focus on justice instead of love, we currently err toward innocence. We may be innocent—*but we are in error.*

Getting Back onto the Tightrope

As long as our entire focus is on harvesting, as long as our entire focus is on courageous proclamation of truth without regard for the response of our listeners, we can continue to ignore shrewdness. We can speak to unbelievers without any tiresome effort to understand them. We can preach the same way to them as we do in church on a Sunday morning.

But if we want to begin to sow, if we want to communicate with art and not just science, if we want to become insiders and work toward positions of influence and respect in the world, we *must* begin "Pursuing Personal Shrewdness." I don't use that title in jest. The pursuit of personal *holiness* has an entire movement that surrounds and encourages it: books, tapes, discussion groups, etc. The pursuit of prudence, sensibility, and practical wisdom will require no less.

How can I show through my words and my actions that I respect what is right in the sight of other people, and yet still seek to persuade them? The answers to these questions require more than biblical knowledge—they require practical wisdom. The Wisconsin legislature turned out to be a difficult place to harvest, but it would have been a wonderful place to sow. Reggie White has all the courage he needs; now he needs the fellowship of shrewd, experienced Christians who can help him present his message wisely to an unbelieving audience. In other words, he needs to learn to sow.

And so do we.

Chapter 8 | A TIME TO SOW

As we saw in John 4, Jesus made it clear that He was sending His disciples to harvest where others had sown, and He implied that the disciples' success would be the result of a team effort. Their fruitful harvest would be made possible by the hard, behind-the-scenes work of unknown laborers who had come before them. The disciples had no way of knowing who the harvesters were or what they had actually contributed; but one day, Jesus said, the sowers and the harvesters would celebrate the success of their joint venture together.

Sowing, we've said, is the long, slow, behind-the-scenes process of preparing an individual, or an entire culture, to be able to hear and believe the gospel. The sower works to create an atmosphere—a soil, if you will—that is conducive to the growth of the gospel. If the sower does his work well—what Jesus referred to as "the *hard* work"—then the harvester may find an abundant harvest awaiting him. If the sower *doesn't* do his job, the harvester may find himself casting his pearls before swine. Jesus was the greatest harvester of all, but even Jesus was preceded by John the Baptist, whose job was to "make ready the way of the Lord" (Matthew 3:3). Why did Jesus need to have His way made ready? How would Jesus have been received if John had failed to do his job?

Harvesting and sowing are not two contradictory methods of evangelism vying for supremacy, but two *complementary roles*, each with its own focus and methodology. The following chart summarizes the different concerns of the sower and harvester.

The harvester focuses on . . .	While the sower focuses on . . .
The End Result	Preparing the Way
Proclamation	Persuasion
Immediate Results	Gradual Change
Individual Effort	Team Impact
Points of Disagreement	Common Ground
Answers	Questions
Justice	Love
Courage	Wisdom
Innocence	Shrewdness

I've been involved in a ministry of evangelism for more than twenty years, and I've watched a change take place during that time that is a cause for great concern.

A Less Abundant Harvest

Almost thirty years ago, as a young college student and a *very* new Christian, I was trained in the basic principles of evangelism. I learned to present the gospel using a simple tract, the Four Spiritual Laws. I discussed that little booklet with roommates, fraternity members, grad students, international students, and even professors. I presented the gospel to literally *hundreds* of people during my four years of college, and I found a tremendous amount of openness—even eagerness—to discuss spiritual things. In those days, I could *assume* the openness of the average hearer. My sole filter when considering a potential listener was, "Are you busy?" Today, many Christians attempting to do evangelism find that they now must assume the disinterest, or even the *hostility*, of the average hearer. As a result, the statistics on evangelistic success from most ministries are much lower than they were thirty years ago.

What accounts for this change? Our first instinct has been to examine ourselves. Have we lost our first love? Are we lacking in dedication or commitment? Are we as bold as we used to be? Our second response has been to reconsider our methodology. Is this booklet out-of-date? Are we behind the times? Should we expand this, enlarge this, reprint it in four-color, or make it available on CD-ROM? The option we rarely consider—perhaps because it sounds *unspiritual*—is that times have changed. Perhaps our nation has entered a different phase of the harvest cycle. Perhaps our culture's fields are not as ripe as they used to be.

In John 4, Jesus uttered His famous words, "I tell you, open your eyes and look at the fields! They are ripe for harvest" (v. 35 NIV). Christians have often assumed that Jesus was stating a timeless spiritual principle: Now that the Messiah has come, a new era has begun. The fields will *always* be white for harvest. Is that what Jesus was saying? If so, He picked a strange metaphor. In actual farming, a time of harvest is followed by a time of rest, followed by a time of sowing, and the process begins all over again. In farming, *no* field is *always* ripe for harvest. Was Jesus telling us that His fields were different, in that they were *always* ripe? Or was He telling His disciples something about the day in which *they* lived? "But when the fullness of the time came," Galatians tells us, "God sent forth His Son . . ." (4:4). Much has been written about the "fullness of the time" and why the Messiah came when He did. Could it be that a part of the "fullness of the time" was that the fields of Jesus' time had been thoroughly sown and were now abundantly—perhaps *uniquely*—ripe for harvest?

No one can deny that the apostolic age was a remarkable period of harvest. But would anyone claim that the fields of Palestine have always been equally ripe ever since—even today? Near the end of the apostolic age, the Jewish Christians were dispersed, and the harvest shifted from Palestine into the Roman Empire itself. As the Empire declined, the harvest began to move into Europe. Spiritually speaking, our planet operates like one giant farm planted with a vast variety of crops. One field ripens while another lies fallow. One field produces an abundant harvest, sometimes followed by a period of dormancy—or even sterility. Many cultures throughout history have been remarkably open to the gospel during one season only to be incredibly resistant later on. The Germany of Martin Luther was not the same as the Germany of Adolph Hitler.

I believe that one of the reasons American ministries enjoyed such evangelistic success thirty years ago is that our culture's fields, much like the fields of Jesus' day, were abundantly white for harvest. I believe they were operating at the peak of a harvest cycle. Consider for a moment just a few of the forces that were working together to create the American culture in 1960, which had a climate of spiritual openness. Consider also how different that culture is today.

1960: Television was dominated by just three networks, wrote Newsweek international editor Michael Elliott, "which became the great postwar mass cultural phenomenon, so that everyone watched 'I Love Lucy' and 'The Honeymooners.'"

Today: "That's inconceivable now," Elliott wrote. "Today you couldn't possibly create the conditions in which people have precisely the same cultural references."[1]

1960: In the 1950s, there was no significant immigration to the United States, creating a highly unified society.

Today: Within a few years, more than half of America's population growth will be due to immigration, creating a highly diverse society.

1960: America was a "melting pot" of different ethnic groups.

Today: More and more ethnic groups strive to maintain their cultural and religious identities within American borders.

1960: Americans had great respect for the clergy and thought of America as a Christian nation.

Today: In the wake of several televangelist and ministry scandals, Americans distrust the clergy and view America as a pluralistic nation.

1960:   As a response to the rampant materialism of the fifties, young people rejected materialism and worldly possessions.

Today: As a response to the rampant materialism of the eighties, young people are quite comfortable with worldly possessions.

1960:   Vietnam became the defining event of the young generation, becoming a unifying theme and rallying point.

Today: There is no defining event, unifying theme, or rallying point for the young.

It's not hard to see why the culture of the sixties was in many ways better prepared to consider the gospel than the culture of today.

What does the farmer do when his fields are ripe? He harvests, and harvest is what we did in the sixties. But what does the farmer do when his fields are no longer ripe? *He sows*, and that is precisely what we must now do to prepare for the next abundant harvest—and to avoid the spiritual famine that will result if we do not.

A Smaller Harvest Field

Let me state my concern plainly. Because we enjoyed such evangelistic success in the sixties, we told ourselves that the American fields would *always* be white for harvest. Because harvesting was so effective, we told ourselves that harvesting was the only technique we would *ever* need. If the fields are eternally ripe, we only need to harvest. Why bother with anything else?

So we teach each new generation of Christians how to harvest —*only* how to harvest—and we assure them that the fields around them are ripe and ready for the picking, if only they will have the faith and the boldness to go. Our books and our training videos are loaded with illustrations that show how easy it is and how open people are to hearing the gospel. But when they go, they sometimes have a rude awakening. The fields around them do *not* always seem ripe. People are not as eager and open as they expected—sometimes they're even hostile. And so, because harvesting is all they know how to do, they begin to withdraw from the fields.

Suppose your pastor preaches on the need for every Christian to witness of his faith and to reach out to his neighbors right where he lives. You return home, duly convicted and motivated to witness. But where do you begin? You consider the families around you. The family to your left is Hindu. The woman to your right is a radical feminist, with a placard by the front door that reads, "A woman without a man is like a fish without a bicycle." The man across the street has a car with a bumper sticker on the back: a fish that contains the name "Darwin" is consuming a little fish with a cross inside. Down the street lives a different sort of couple—a married couple with 1.2 children, college educated, and conservative in their values.

With whom do you think you'll attempt to share your faith? Much more importantly: *What will you say to everyone else?*

The problem is not simply that we fear talking with people who are so unlike us. *The problem is what we think of when we think of sharing our faith.* Because we think exclusively in terms of harvesting, the thought process that goes through our minds is, *I can't harvest with a Hindu, or a feminist, or an evolutionist, so I guess I'll try to harvest with the Young Republicans.* The tragic result is that we attempt to share the faith with those we think may be closest to it and say nothing to everyone else.

I recently heard a minister say, "We don't have time to try to *make* people interested in spiritual things. We need to find the people who are *already* interested and talk to *them*." An African-American friend of mine quipped, "It's a funny thing. To white people, African Americans *never* look interested."

Can you see the change that has taken place? Evangelism used to be a process of taking the gospel into untouched places and to un-reached people. Today, because we insist on harvesting alone, and be-cause harvesting is getting harder to do, we are saying nothing at all to more and more people. We are withdrawing from the resistant and stubborn people who might need more time and more convincing —the vast majority of Americans. We spend our time instead with a rapidly shrinking minority, the people who are "ready to listen"— people like us. This allows the Hindu, feminist, and evolutionist to go their separate ways with no communication whatsoever from the Christian next door. As this continues to happen on a larger and larger scale, our country begins to polarize into two distinct spheres: the Christian and the *definitely* non-Christian.

That is *exactly* the situation we have in our society today, and I believe most Christians are unaware of the great danger this situation presents. A generation ago our nation was similarly divided into the Christian and the non-Christian, but most non-Christians were at least friendly to and respectful of the gospel. Today, with less and less communication from the Christian world, true nonbelievers are free to grow more ignorant, more distant, and more *hostile*.

Broadening Our Field of Labor

What can we do to help reverse this dangerous polarization? What can we do to reach out not only to those who are *like* us, but also to those who are most *unlike* us? We can begin to think in a different way about communicating our faith. When we think of communicating with those around us, we can begin to use *this* thought process: *I may not be able to harvest yet with the Hindu, the feminist, or the evolutionist. But what can I say to each of them? Where can I at least begin? How can I sow?*

Because times have changed, fewer Americans today may be receptive to a complete presentation of the gospel. It's not as easy as it used to be to say *everything*—but that doesn't mean you can't say *anything*. I may not be able to harvest exactly as I did thirty years ago, but I can say *something* to everybody I meet. That's what sowing is all about. The sower looks at his neighborhood, office, or campus and sees a harvest of fruit. He knows that some of the fruit in his field is ripe now, and he must find it before it spoils. He also knows that much of the fruit is not yet ripe, and some plants are far too immature to bear fruit at all. As a sower, he knows that there is *something* he can do to encourage the growth of *every* plant in his field, and none of his efforts are wasted. Even if he doesn't see the fruit of his labor, he knows that someone else may.

Where does the sower begin his work?

As strange as it may sound, the first thing every new farmer must do is not plant or water, but build fences. In other words, he must define the limits of his daily responsibility. *This* land belongs to me; *that* land does not. In the same way, the starting point for every sower is to define his "turf." Who are the people with whom you regularly come in contact? Think carefully through the people you encounter in an average week: the neighbors, car-pool members, co-workers, store clerks, etc. Work from the first person you see each day —perhaps the neighbor you greet when you fetch the morning paper —to the last person you encounter each night—the fellow parent you stand beside as you watch your daughter's soccer practice. These people represent your turf, the fields in which you have the opportunity to practice the sower's art.

With this introductory step completed, the sower is now ready to enter his fields. What exactly does the sower *do?* What are the tools that make up his toolbox? As we'll see in the next chapters, the sower's world consists of three basic activities: He cultivates, he plants, and he nurtures.

Chapter 9 | CULTIVATING THE SOIL

During the seven-year period from 1933 to 1939, one of the worst environmental disasters in world history took place—not on the shorelines of Alaska, or in the rain forests of the Amazon, but in the heartland of America.

It was a tragedy so great that it defies comprehension: a hundred *million* acres of ruined or endangered land; once-fertile grasslands now scorched and barren; houses flattened and buried under tons of silt; an apocalyptic landscape littered with the skeletal remains of starving livestock and rusting farm machinery.

In 1931, a drought began in the Great Plains states. The sweeping winds that signaled each spring shrieked across the prairie. Storm after storm swept through, stripping away the precious few inches of life-sustaining topsoil. In one storm alone, 350 million tons of dirt— enough to bury all of Chicago a foot deep—were lifted into the sky and deposited as far away as the Atlantic coast. Sand drifted in great heaps; it choked machinery, covered roads, and mounded in massive dunes. The Great Prairies were now christened with a new name: the Dust Bowl. The prairie farmer, in his eagerness for profit and ignorance of the ancient grasslands, had drained the soil of its very ability to sustain life. The land was dead.

Fortunately, the federal government understood that a hundred million acres of American heartland could not simply be discarded. In 1935, the Soil Conservation Service was created to teach farmers how to give back to the land. By 1941, millions of damaged and endangered acres had been effectively reclaimed. The Soil Conservation Service taught farmers much more than principles of soil conservation; it taught a philosophy of the soil. It helped farmers to think about the soil in a different way, to understand that our rocky and lifeless earth is covered by only a few precious inches of life-supporting topsoil. Soil is itself a crop; it must be cultivated and tended just as carefully as the harvest it produces.

Cultivating is the process of preparing the soil to sustain life. Agronomists say that the ideal soil contains equal parts of clay, sand, and organic material. In addition, the soil must maintain a proper level of acidity and moisture content. If any of these elements are deficient, plant what you will—nothing will grow.

Today's Deficient Soil

The sower recognizes that certain soil elements are necessary for a person to be able to understand and believe the gospel. As Jesus said, there are good soils and bad soils, and each age has its characteristic soil deficiencies that challenge the sowing of the gospel. In our day there are six common deficiencies that a good sower must learn to recognize and remedy before the gospel can take root.

Soil Deficiency 1: Ignorance of All Things Biblical

The authors of *What Do Our 17-Year-Olds Know?* described the results of a national assessment of the knowledge of high school juniors in the areas of history and literature. They found that 40 percent of students thought that Jonah was thrown into a lion's den, or that he was shipwrecked on an island, or that he killed a giant. Thirty percent of students thought that Jesus was betrayed by Pilate, or the apostle John—or even by Mary.[1] Some of pollster George Barna's findings are even more discouraging. Ninety percent of Americans cannot define the term "Great Commission," only a third of adults know the meaning of the expression "the gospel," and despite repeated exposure at major sporting events, 70 percent of Americans have no idea what is meant by "John 3:16." "As a nation," Barna concluded, "our understanding of God, Jesus Christ, the Christian faith, the Bible and critical concepts such as salvation by grace are a mile wide and an inch deep."[2]

The increasing biblical ignorance in America has one very serious consequence. In more and more cases, when Christians try to witness to non-Christians, *the non-Christians have no idea what we're talking about.* Talking to an American about the Bible is now a cross-cultural experience.

An undergraduate student at Harvard University once decided to conduct an informal study in communication on the streets of Cambridge. He casually approached random passersby and asked, "Can you tell me how to get to Central Square?" The typical response was very brief, giving no more information than was necessary. "Go two blocks; turn left." When the student approached other passersby, he prefaced his question by saying, "I'm from out of town." Sometimes he even tried to speak in an unfamiliar accent. In these cases, the locals went to great lengths to give thorough directions, describing landmarks along the way and telling him how he would recognize Central Square when he got there.[3]

The citizens of Cambridge intuitively understood a basic principle of human communication: *The less knowledge a person has in common with us, the more carefully and thoroughly we must communicate with him.* Strangely, modern Christians rarely apply that principle when communicating with nonbelievers. We forget that, when it comes to all things biblical, most Americans are from out of town. We sound like insensitive locals, impatiently repeating the same brief instructions over and over to a frustrated and embarrassed tourist. "No, no, no! By *grace* you have been *saved* through *faith* . . ." As modern Christians seek to communicate with this generation, we need to remember that the soil of common knowledge has been depleted.

The sower's job is to supplement the soil; she must try to determine the limits of her listener's biblical knowledge so that she will know how far back her dialogue needs to begin. In our conversations with non-Christians today, we sometimes assume far more understanding than they actually possess. Your listener may be so spiritually ignorant that the gospel would sound virtually meaningless to her.

In case you think that's an exaggeration, consider *my* story. When I was a senior in high school, I had never opened a Bible in my life. One day it occurred to me that I should check it out, so I dug my grandmother's crusty, dusty copy from the closet. I flipped it open at random and was greeted by the word "Job" at the top of the page. Having no need for a job, I flipped to another section. "Habakkuk 2:10" it said. I couldn't even pronounce it. And what's with these numbers? A two, followed by a colon, followed by a ten. I had never seen such a notation in my life. How could I? That notation is unique to religious literature. It occurred to me that perhaps the Bible was somehow mixed in with these other topics. I flipped through the pages, looking for something that said "Bible." Nothing did, of course, so I put the mysterious book away, and that's the last time I opened a Bible until I became a Christian.

If you had asked me "Have you ever read Luke?" I would have said, "Luke who?" If you had told me to look up John 3:16, I would have looked at you with the same blank stare that *you* give when you turn on your computer and see "SYSTEM ERROR F002." The words *sin, salvation, justification,* and *redemption* were not in my vocabulary. What would you say to someone like me? Where would you begin? What words would you use? Those are the questions the sower has to answer. Thirty years ago, my level of ignorance was unusual; today it's common. The sower can help to supplement the soil by assuming nothing about the listener's background knowledge and by adding to his biblical understanding on a gradual basis.

What would that look like? Several years ago my colleagues and I at the Communication Center produced a series of small-group discussion materials intended for the average non-Christian college student. We called them *LifeSkills.* Each discussion dealt with a topic of interest to students and gradually introduced them to a Christian perspective on the topic. Each time a biblical quotation appeared, we were careful to provide a context for the quotation with a simple explanation like this:

• The book of Genesis is the first of the sixty six books that make up the Bible. It has much to say about the nature of life and relationships.

- The book of Galatians was a letter written almost 2,000 years ago. It describes the great freedom that can be found in a relationship with God.

- The book of Philippians was a letter written to Christians in the ancient Roman city of Philippi. It explains how to remain joyful despite the difficult circumstances of life.

- The book of First Corinthians is the first of two letters written by the apostle Paul to Christians who lived in the ancient city of Corinth, Greece. The people of Corinth had a reputation in the ancient world as an unruly, hard-drinking, sexually promiscuous bunch of people. Paul wrote to his friends to remind them of how God expects them to love one another.

Consider how much biblical knowledge a newcomer to the Bible could gain from just the four examples above, all taken from a single *LifeSkills* discussion. *The Bible is not just a book, but a collection of sixty-six separate books. Genesis is the first one. Some of the others aren't really books, but letters named after ancient cities. Some of the letters are two thousand years old, and the people back then were a lot like they are now. The Bible is about some pretty practical stuff.* That's not bad for an hour-long discussion, but it's not information overload. With that much help, I could have opened my grandmother's Bible back in high school and not been frightened away by "Habakkuk." Consider how much more helpful this approach is to the ignorant listener than to simply stand before him and recite, "John 3:16 tells us that 'God so loved the world ...'"

The goal of the *LifeSkills* series was to gradually increase the biblical understanding of the students. The group leader's goal was to try to determine, by the group's questions and interaction, when they were ready for a direct discussion of the gospel—when they were ready to harvest. On occasion the group was ready all at the same time; more often, individuals would indicate their readiness, and the group leader would simply meet with them one-on-one. This is the sower's approach; he cultivates, he plants, and he nurtures, all the time looking for ripe fruit.

What does it mean to your co-worker when you tell her you're a "Presbyterian"? What does she think you mean when you use the word *gospel*—isn't that a kind of music? What would you say to a neighbor if you could no longer use the words *share, witness, saved, sanctified,* or a thousand other words that have lost their meaning to modern hearers? With every person you meet, what can you say *right now* to move him a little farther along on the path to the harvest?

Soil Deficiency 2: Prejudice

A "Far Side" cartoon by Gary Larson features "the Blob family at home." Mama Blob, Papa Blob, and Baby Blob are all watching TV as a smiling, Bible-toting couple approaches the front door. Mama Blob shouts, "Jehovah's Witnesses! Jehovah's Witnesses! Everyone act like beanbag chairs!" It seems like almost everyone today has had some encounter with religious "proselytizing," from a knock at the front door to a request for funds at the local airport. The image of these encounters portrayed in the media is always negative: a lengthy, boring, irrelevant, unwanted intrusion by a glassy-eyed, too-friendly, Scripture-quoting devotee of some religious sect. Thanks to these images, even those who have never had the direct experience *feel* as if they have.

When many evangelistic organizations began their ministries forty or fifty years ago, aggressive evangelism was a novel experience—especially in places like a college campus. The Four Spiritual Laws booklet, created by Campus Crusade in the early sixties, was practically a new form of communication. In those days, when you pulled out a tract to show to someone, the response was often, "Look at that! It's like a little book, only smaller. It's a sort of book*let*." The Four Spiritual Laws is an outstanding tool that God has used in tremendous ways all over the world—but we need to remember that more than 2.5 *billion* copies of the Four Spiritual Laws have been distributed, and today the tract has become a virtual *symbol* of religious persuasion. Because of this level of exposure, even those who have never actually read a tract think they know what's in them.

In the act of cultivating, the sower has to plow through far more stubborn, encrusted prejudice than in years past. There have always been stumbling blocks to the gospel, but in the past most of them have been related to the gospel itself; today some of the biggest stumbling blocks are simply the *stereotypes* and *images* of Christians. Some of the biggest barriers to belief are not about reality, but about perceptions.

I once asked the students at the Communication Center to describe for me the stereotype of an evangelical Christian in the eyes of the average American. Here is a part of their list:

- Phony
- Pushy
- Manipulative
- Politically conservative
- Socially conservative

- Intolerant
- Know-it-alls
- Out of touch
- Out of date
- No sense of humor

That's just a *partial* list. Unfortunately, perceptions like these often shape the way people think and respond. "I'm not concerned about the way things *are*," wrote the philosopher Epictetus, "but about the way men *think* things are." A non-Christian who believes that *all* Christians are phony, pushy, manipulative, and intolerant will have a hard time ever hearing the gospel. Who would he listen to? That's why the sower has to spend time working to break the unbeliever's stereotypes so that he'll be *able* to listen.

How is this done? A simple look at the Christian stereotype list above suggests some possibilities.

- *Don't be pushy or manipulative.* Don't feel that every conversation with your neighbor must be turned to spiritual issues. Don't insist on forcing the harvest even when the fruit is not yet ripe.

- *Don't voice all your political viewpoints.* Your co-worker doesn't have to know how you feel about welfare reform, capital punishment, and Rush Limbaugh. And maybe it's better that he doesn't, if you want to talk about God later.

- *Don't know everything.* On some subjects, withhold your opinion. Tell him you're still thinking about it. Ask him for his. This shouldn't be false humility either—you don't know everything, and he can teach you something.

- *Stay in touch.* Who won the World Series this year? What was on TV last night? Do you care about anything that he cares about—or are you so heavenly minded that you're of no earthly good?

• *Lighten up.* Nothing shatters the stereotype of arrogance and stuffiness as fast as the ability to laugh—especially at yourself.

Soil Deficiency 3: Personal Issues

In the parable of the sower, Jesus portrayed a man "on whom seed was sown among the thorns." The thorns are "the worries of this life, the deceitfulness of wealth and the desires for other things" (Mark 4:19 NIV). These worries and desires come in and *choke* the Word; like actual thorns, they grow in size until they literally suck the life out of the plant itself.

It would be a much better world if people could hear the gospel in a vacuum. Sheltered and protected from the cares and concerns of daily life, they could listen without interruption and consider the issues without distraction. Unfortunately, that world does not exist, and *no one* hears the gospel that way. As Jesus' parable suggested, the Word is sown in the midst of confusion, affliction, persecution, and worry—and these things *greatly* affect how that Word will be received.

In fact, Jesus' brief list of "thorns" in the parable of the sower could be expanded. The Scriptures suggest several other things that also have the power to choke the soil around us. An expanded list might include things like:

• Anxiety and worry
• The cares and demands of life
• Materialism and greed
• Sexual lust
• Pride and the desire for power
• Immorality and unrighteousness
• Relational problems

Given the pressures of modern life, I think it's safe to assume that *everyone* struggles with at least one of the above temptations. That means that the Word is *always* sown in the presence of thorns and is always in danger of being choked—squeezed out of the conscious mind of the listener by more pressing issues. The job of the sower, then, is to recognize the personal issues that might be distracting the listener and to clear the soil of thorns in preparation for planting.

A new family recently moved into our neighborhood from Germany. The husband speaks excellent English, and his wife is just barely conversant. Their four children, on the other hand, didn't speak a *word* of English when they came—and yet they began public school in the fall alongside all the other neighborhood kids. Can you imagine what it would be like to sit in a class and not understand a *single word* that's being said? I came close to that experience once in a physics class, and it was frightening. A few weeks ago my wife and I invited the family to church—but not for the reason you might think. Our church was hosting a choir visiting from Germany, and we invited our neighbors simply to give them a chance to speak their own language for a few minutes with someone who could understand.

It could have been impossible to relate to our new neighbors about spiritual issues while they were struggling under such enormous daily pressure. What about the people on *your* turf? Are you aware of their "worries of this life," or are you attempting to plant seed in soil already choked with thorns?

As you listen carefully to the woman waiting with you at the kids' bus stop, ask yourself:

- Is there a topic that seems to occupy a majority of her attention?
- Is there a subject that seems to generate an unusual amount of anger or anxiety for her?
- How does she talk about her husband and her marriage?
- How are her children doing? Does any one of them seem to cause her special concern?
- Does she ever hint—or even joke—about any hidden longings, desires, or regrets?

Soil Deficiency 4: An Inadequate Worldview

In an old "Twilight Zone" episode a man is sentenced to die in the electric chair. As he is dragged kicking and screaming from the courtroom, he shouts, "Don't you understand? I'm the only one who actually exists! You are all the product of my imagination. If I die, you'll all cease to exist too!" For some reason, this strange line of reasoning gets under the skin of the prosecuting attorney, who visits the prisoner on death row. The prisoner explains further. The attorney wrestles with his bizarre claim, but he is never quite convinced. In the end, the prisoner dies—and everyone else vanishes along with him. Next stop: the Twilight Zone.

An actual philosophy known as solipsism holds that the self is the only thing that can be known and verified. Needless to say, a solipsist would be extremely skeptical about most things—perhaps everything outside of himself. There are many things he simply *could not* believe; his worldview would make it impossible.

Our world has many solipsists. Convicted murderers sometimes show no remorse whatsoever for their actions. It's as though the victim—and the victim's family—did not actually exist. New programs are now arranging meetings between the murderer and the victim's family so that the killer can experience firsthand the enormous pain and loss the family has experienced. Through this encounter, some murderers actually gain the ability to experience guilt and remorse for the first time. The goal of the program is simple: To desire repentance you must feel guilt; to feel guilt you must believe something was wrong; to believe something was wrong you must experience the pain you caused. Each belief is supported by a prior belief.

In chapter 2 we looked at certain prior beliefs that are necessary before the gospel *can* be embraced. Some of those necessary prior beliefs include:

- Our five senses can be trusted.
- Miracles could occur.
- There might be a spiritual world.
- History can be known.
- There might be absolute truths.
- Words convey an author's meaning.

Unfortunately, in our postmodern age many of these very beliefs are being challenged. The result is that today, many of our listeners lack the basic beliefs necessary to understand and accept the gospel. The problem is not with the gospel itself; the soil is simply too thin to support the weight of the plant.

I once attempted to have a spiritual conversation with a man who was absolutely convinced that history was one vast, muddled mess. He was adamant that nothing can be known about the past before this century and that nothing was certain except what he himself could experience firsthand. Needless to say, he was not at all open to the gospel. How could he be? If history can't be known, there goes the Incarnation, the Crucifixion, the Resurrection, and the Bible itself. What's left? Faced with this kind of roadblock, many Christians simply "testify." "I'll push ahead with the gospel anyway," they might reason, "and what he does with it is up to him." But what's the point? With his inadequate worldview, he *cannot* believe it. Why not recite it in French?

The sower's response is to take the time to address the faulty worldview. In this case, I asked the man why he drew the line at *this* century. If he only trusted things he could experience firsthand, *nothing* could be known except the things he was experiencing at that very moment. The *entire* past was lost to him; he couldn't even be certain about what he had for breakfast that morning. He began to see that there were a number of things that he felt quite certain about that had happened before that moment. That was as far as our conversation went. When I left, he was beginning to reconsider his view of history. To the sower, that represents a victory. Though I saw no conversion that day, I may have made a contribution toward an eventual harvest.

The biggest objection to this principle is that it takes so much *time*. We can't spend countless hours with every individual we meet, repairing every inadequate worldview so that *someday* we can finally share the gospel with *someone*. No, we can't. But every Christian can learn to recognize when there is a *fatal flaw* in a listener's worldview—a flaw that renders belief in the gospel impossible. At that point, the Christian has three choices: He can break off the conversation, he can uselessly attempt to force the harvest, *or he can sow*. I believe that sowing is the wisest investment.

Soil Deficiency 5: Cultural Issues

A famous study was done in Milwaukee during the early 1950s, what we now refer to as the McCarthy Era or the era of the Red Scare. Accusations of Communist sympathy were pointed everywhere, and suspected people often found themselves out of a job and unable to get one. During that time there was a pervasive, almost tangible atmosphere of fear in our country, and a reporter decided to test its extent. He made up a petition; at the top was a simple statement of human rights. He stopped passersby in the downtown area and asked them to read the statement. If they agreed in principle, he asked them to sign the petition. Out of a hundred men and women who read the statement, not one would sign his or her name to the petition. Ironically, the statement was just a portion of the U.S. Constitution.

What would prevent an American from signing his name to his own Constitution? A cultural atmosphere of fear: the concern that a person's name, appearing in the wrong place, could cost him his job. Though we no longer live in the McCarthy Era, culture-wide attitudes and values still influence how people think—and how they might respond to the gospel.

Books on cultural trends abound, but consider just a few societal attitudes that culture watchers have observed in the last few years that could greatly affect the reception of the gospel.

- Deeply imbedded skepticism
- Insistence on privacy
- Resistance to persuasion
- Relativistic view of truth
- High value on tolerance
- Commitment to diversity

I live in North Carolina. Our soil here consists largely of red clay. Clay tends to be naturally acidic, so some plants (like azaleas) flourish, whereas others (like my front lawn) struggle to survive. My next-door neighbor has exactly the same soil; so does most everyone living in the Southeastern United States. In fact, anyone moving to my area can expect the same soil conditions, and every new homeowner will take those conditions into account when he selects the flowers and shrubs to plant in his yard—if he wants them to grow.

The sower must ask questions like these: "Are there *culture-wide* soil conditions? Are there attitudes toward the gospel that I can expect simply because I live in America at the start of a new millennium? Have the soil conditions *changed* in recent years? How have they changed? How do they appear to be changing as I look toward the future?" The answers to these questions will help the sower determine what he can say—and how he had better say it.

When a fund-raiser knocks at my door at dinnertime I feel violated—my privacy has been invaded and I'm immediately defensive. When a salesman tells me, "I'm not here to sell you anything," I'm suspicious—I'm resistant to persuasion. When a commercial presents the glowing virtues of a political candidate, I'm doubtful—I'm instinctively skeptical. I haven't escaped the effect of our culture's soil conditions, and neither have you—or your listeners. A sower's mindset will help us communicate in a way that fits the times we live in.

Soil Deficiency 6: Personal Cost

The story is told of a chicken and a pig who decided to have breakfast together. "Why don't we go out for some bacon and eggs?" suggested the chicken. "No, thanks," said the pig. "For you, bacon and eggs is just a contribution. For me it's a total commitment."

The price of Christian faith is not the same for everyone on our planet. My son will apply for college soon, and he will proudly list his church involvement on his application form, expecting it to increase his chances of acceptance. That same admission in a Muslim country could increase his chances of imprisonment or even death.

Jesus once warned His disciples, "I did not come to bring peace, but a sword" (Matthew 10:34). Jesus said that His life and teachings would not be a unifying point that would finally bring peace to a troubled world. On the contrary, faith in Christ would become a dividing point that in some cases would even tear families apart.

Jesus "brings the sword" in varying degrees to each new believer's life, and He warned new believers to "count the cost" before signing up. It's a wise sower who realizes that the potential cost of belief is not the same for everyone; it's an even wiser sower who takes the time to understand the specific price tag attached to each individual life. Consider just a few of the possible costs involved in coming to Christ:

- *Religious costs.* A Buddhist who becomes a Christian may barely raise an eyebrow. An orthodox Jew who is baptized as a Christian may find that his family has hosted his funeral. Does your listener come from a specific religious background? What would it cost him to "change horses in midstream"?

- *Family costs.* Jesus said, "I came to set a man against his father, and a daughter against her mother, and a daughter-in-law against her mother-in-law; and a man's enemies will be the members of his household" (Matthew 10:35–36). Sometimes a change in faith can cause the wrath of parents, children, or in-laws.

- *Marital costs.* Paul cautioned Christians not to be unequally yoked with unbelievers. When we invite a husband or wife to individually receive Christ, we *create* an unequal yoking that may cause a serious marital rift.

- *Business costs.* When Zaccheus accepted Christ it cost him half of his possessions and a fourfold penalty to everyone he had defrauded. Faith in Christ could greatly change the way your listener conducts his business; it could even cost him his job.

- *Friendship costs.* Sometimes your listener suspects—quite rightly—that he can *either* become a Christian *or* keep his current friends, but he cannot do both. His friends just might be the cost of belief.

- *Lifestyle costs.* When Jesus told the rich young ruler to "sell all that you possess and distribute it to the poor," the young man "became very sad, for he was extremely rich" (Luke 18:22–23). What would have to change in the listener's manners, morals, and money if he became a Christian? What might he have to give up?

It's important to note that Jesus followed His words, "I came to set a man against his father" with the words, "He who loves father or mother more than Me is not worthy of Me" (Matthew 10:37). Jesus knew that faith in Him could involve a price, but He fully expected us to pay that price—no matter how great. The sower should never withhold the gospel because the potential cost looks too great. Every individual must make that decision for himself. But the sower *should* try to understand just how great the price of belief is for his listener so he can have a sense of what he is really asking, and so he can lend the support necessary to help the listener make such a costly decision.

Analyzing the Soil

The sower's first job is to cultivate the soil—to work in the listener's life to create an atmosphere where belief is at least *possible*. She does this by learning to recognize the six soil deficiencies that are common to our day, and then supplementing the soil in the specific area of weakness. But how does the sower analyze the soil? Simply through conversation—and not necessarily about spiritual issues. General, day-to-day conversation can tell you a lot about a person's attitudes and beliefs. Listen to a few snippets from daily conversations, and see if you can recognize the soil deficiency suggested by each.

- Did you hear the joke about the little kid who was talking to his grandma about church? He said, "It doesn't matter where we go to church, does it, Grandma, as long as we're all Republicans?" Isn't that the truth!
- My husband grew up going to church, and he hated it. He says the next time he goes it'll be in a coffin.
- I think we could do away with half of the intolerance in the country if we could just get rid of these right-wing fundamentalists.
- Where I work, you do what you're told. And if you have to bend the rules a little, you just do it—if you want to keep your job.
- Can you believe that salesman? He was as pushy as an evangelist.

To cultivate the soil takes time. But instead of thinking of cultivating as a long, drawn-out practice with one listener at a time, think of it as something you do every day, with everyone you meet. I have a conversation here, I chat for a few minutes there, all the time listening for the telltale signs of a soil deficiency. I make a comment here, I ask a pointed question there, I break a stereotype along the way. With everyone I meet I am cultivating the soil and improving the climate for spiritual growth. With everyone I meet I am gently tugging at the vine, looking for the signs of ripe fruit.

And once the soil is cultivated and ready, it's time for the sower's next responsibility: to plant the seed.

Chapter 10 | # PLANTING PART 1— THE THREE TOOLS

L ife today seems to be enormously complex, either by nature or by our own design. Everyone lives with some level of distraction, and that distraction makes it difficult to get beyond the cares of *this* world long enough to consider the possibility of a world to come.

The best example of the distraction principle can be found at municipal airports. There, you may encounter a member of some Eastern religious movement who is attempting to stop hurrying passengers to discuss spiritual matters and hopefully raise a few dollars on the side. He stands at a busy intersection, a canvas bag draped from one shoulder, holding up colorful books featuring bald-headed men as he smiles and calls out to one bustling traveler after another. "Hi, where are you headed this afternoon?" "Hello there, do you have a minute to . . ." "Hi, have you ever . . ." "Excuse me, I . . ." One after another the travelers race by, carefully avoiding eye contact, and often pretending the solicitor doesn't even exist. I've watched passengers walk well out of their way just to avoid a possible encounter with one of these spiritual advisers.

Can you blame the passengers? I've often joked that at the airport, even people who don't smoke start smoking. Can you imagine a more frantic, frenzied, frenetic place? Your plane was thirty minutes late. You now have only fifteen minutes to make your connection, and it's at the other end of the airport. You have two massive carry-on bags, and the shoulder strap just broke on one of them. You really ought to stop and call your wife and tell her you might be late, but is there time? Why won't the lady in front of you walk faster? Why are there so many children at the airport? Why do people *have* children, anyway?

As you reach the top of the escalator, a smiling figure steps in front of you and extends his hand. "Good morning. Where are you headed today? Have you got a minute?" Have you got a *minute?* Is he *joking?* A minute is the one thing you do *not* have. In fact, for a split second you consider grasping the hand and pulling suddenly, using the momentum to sling you past that woman who is still in front of you.

The solicitor's request seems incredibly out of place. Nowhere are people more distracted than at the airport, and yet this is the setting where the mystic hopes to engage someone in a conversation about his spiritual life. How can anyone be expected to focus on the intangible when the demands of the tangible are all around him?

This problem would be of little concern if it were confined to the airport. The problem is, the airport is a symbol of the average American's lifestyle. We are always going somewhere, always needing to make connections, and always overloaded with baggage. In today's world, the tangible distractions around us are so great that we almost never have time to contemplate the intangible. Have I got a *minute?* Are you *joking?*

Here is a list of a few of the problems an average person might deal with in a normal day. Do they sound familiar?

- I have to get the tires rotated.
- I need to look into refinancing my mortgage while the rates are good.
- I accidentally booked two lunch appointments, and I need to keep them both.
- One of the kids just called from school and said she's sick.

- I have to pick up a prescription, the dry cleaning, and some milk. I think.
- I just ran out of gas.
- I need to consider my eternal destiny.

That last item sounds incredibly out of place, doesn't it? It sounds so philosophical, so otherworldly, so *irrelevant*. Given a choice between picking up a sick daughter from school and considering the gospel, who's going to choose the latter? The problem is, *this is the average American's day*. If the gospel doesn't seem to fit in today, when *does* it fit?

I believe that people are essentially spiritual beings, and we are driven by spiritual needs. "We are not human beings having a spiritual experience," writes Wayne Dyer, "we are spiritual beings having a human experience."[1] The problem is that our human experience is so distracting that the spiritual often has to be *injected* into life, just as a badly needed vaccine must be injected into the blood system. But injections can be painful; the trick is to inject the spiritual into daily life in a way that doesn't seem annoying, abrupt, or insensitive. That's the sower's challenge. That's what it means to plant.

How does the sower accomplish this? When it comes to planting, the first issue to consider is timing. A farmer can have the hardiest seedlings in the world, but if he plants them out of season they won't survive. We can learn an important lesson about timing by remembering the airport. What does our encounter with the Eastern mystic teach us? It teaches us that people are often too busy or distracted to seriously consider spiritual things. What it does *not* teach us is that people are no longer *interested* in spiritual things. The lesson is simply that timing is one important consideration; there are good and bad moments to try to inject the spiritual into a distracted life.

A parent who wants to communicate well with a teenager must be willing to wait for *moments of openness,* undistracted moments when the teenager is willing to interact on a deeper level. These moments may be rare, and parents know that it requires patience and sensitivity to recognize them. But it's worth the wait; at those times, there is an opportunity to communicate about issues much deeper than the superficialities of daily life.

The same principle applies to anyone you meet. There are predictable "open moments" when the average person is commonly more open to consider spiritual issues:

- *Holidays:* Christmas, Easter, New Year's Day, birthdays
- *Transitional events:* A job change, a child going to school, a child leaving home, a move, a fortieth birthday, retirement
- *Family crises:* A child's illness, a surgery or hospitalization, a divorce or separation, a parent-child conflict, the death of a parent or friend, a financial setback
- *National events:* The space shuttle explodes, the president has an affair, the economy is uncertain, everyone is watching the news about another senseless tragedy

There are also open moments that are unique to each individual. Consider your next-door neighbor, for example. When are the best times to try to connect with him at a deeper-than-normal level? It might be when you sit together with him on his deck, or when you're working on something together, or when you're driving somewhere. What are *his* open moments?

To be able to recognize these open moments requires that you actually *know* something about your neighbor and that you actually have such times of interaction with him. That's why the sower, through every daily conversation with everyone he meets, is constantly learning the best time to plant.

But once the sower has decided on the proper timing, what does he use to plant? For the farmer, planting involves placing something very small in the soil—a tiny seed or a shoot—in hopes that, with time, it will grow much larger and produce a return. The sower does the same; when the soil has been cultivated and the timing is right, he begins to implant the Word in the life of his unbelieving friend. There are three specialized tools that the sower can use to help him in this planting process: questions, agreements, and his own life.

Tool #1: Questions

Four hundred years before the time of Christ, a stout, white-haired old man used to spend his day wandering through the marketplace of ancient Athens, striking up conversations with anyone who would listen. His name was Socrates, and he was a big believer in the power of a good question. Socrates believed that the role of a good teacher is not simply to impart information, but to educate through the asking of skillful questions. This style of teaching has come to be known as the Socratic Method.

Strangely, Christians have a difficult time learning this method. I suspect it's because we are, by nature, answer people. Knowing that truth is on our side, we see it as our job to give answers to an ignorant world. You've got questions? We've got answers. The problem is, when we seem to have *all* the answers, we appear to be arrogant and dogmatic, and our listeners become resistant. Socrates took a different approach. Believing that truth was on his side, he saw it as his job to ask questions of a world that thought it knew everything. Though he certainly knew far more than most Athenians—and more than most of *us*—he pretended to be an ignorant man, and he chose to plant by asking questions. I believe there are four great values to this approach.

1. Questions Are Nonthreatening

Although people grow weary of hearing our answers, they will entertain questions all day. To put it another way: Enough of what *you* know, ask me what *I* know. Questions make the listener far more than a listener; she's now an active *participant* in the conversation. Questions have another benefit: They help to lower the listener's defenses. There is an understanding among people that a question is somehow less intentional, less *threatening* than a direct statement. After all, what's the harm in *asking?*

2. Questions Communicate Humility

The problem with the Christian isn't that he has answers; it's that he has *too many* answers. Christians often have deeply held convictions about capital punishment, criminal justice, welfare reform, economics, and political theory. Too often we are convinced that each opinion is *the* truly biblical position. As a result, Christians seem to have a *lot* of opinions, and we're in danger of appearing arrogant and inflexible in an age of tolerance.

At the Communication Center's summer training program, we used to teach our students to handle questions from an audience.

Some student would always ask, "What do I do if I don't know the answer to a question?" I would say, "Try this: '*I don't know*.'" I recommend this tactic not only for the sake of honesty, but because there is great benefit in admitting ignorance—at least *some* ignorance—to a fellow searcher. There's an old saying: "It's always popular to be searching for truth, but it's never popular to find it." By asking questions, the Christian shows that in *some* areas he, too, is a fellow searcher.

3. Questions Allow Listeners to Discover Truth for Themselves

In Judith Guest's novel *Ordinary People*, a young boy is guilt-ridden over the death of his older brother. He is tortured by a sense of guilt, though he cannot understand why. He visits again and again after school with a psychiatrist, who applies the Socratic Method; he asks, he probes, but he never *tells*. At a climactic moment in the story, the young boy comes to a realization: He feels guilty because he believes that *he* should have died instead of his brother. As the boy weeps in the psychiatrist's arms, he pleads, "Why didn't you *tell* me?" The doctor replies, "*You* had to say it." There is great power in the insights we come to on our own—even if we had help getting there. This may be due to the ancient dictum that says, "A person does not believe something because he thinks it is true; he thinks something is true because *he* believes it." A good question allows a listener to provide his *own* answers instead of having to listen to yours.

4. Questions Demand Questions in Return

Conversations operate by unspoken democratic principles. Most mature listeners, after being asked several questions about themselves or their views, sense that it's only fair to ask a question or two in return. "What about you? What do *you* think?" There's nothing like being *asked* for your viewpoint instead of simply offering an unsolicited—and often unwelcome—opinion. But beware: The danger for the Christian is that once he is asked a question he will eagerly lecture until his listener's eyes glaze over.

Of course, not all questions are created equal. The *value* of a question is determined by the *quality* of the question. This is where the sower needs to build skill. Because Christians tend to be answer people, we're not especially skilled at asking *good* questions—questions that aren't simplistic, leading, or downright insulting. Take a look at any basic Bible study guide. Invariably, you'll find at least *some* questions of this caliber: "Read this verse: 'God so loved the world.' Question: *What* did God love?" Anyone who has been a part of a small-group Bible study knows the awkward embarrassment that occurs when a group leader actually looks at a group and asks, "What did you all get for this one?" Is he *serious?* Does he really expect us to *answer* that?

In a courtroom trial, when an attorney is questioning a witness, the opposing attorney may raise objections. He may call out, "Leading question!" or "Asked and answered!" The attorney is complaining that while his opponent has asked an *apparent* question, it isn't really a question at all. "I think Jesus is the Son of God—who do *you* think He is?" In court, a question is supposed to allow the witness the freedom to answer *as he wills.* A good question possesses three qualities: It's intelligent, it's open-ended, and it raises a point without being manipulative.

Let me suggest four categories of questions that the sower may find helpful, and some specific examples of each.

1. Questions About the Listener's Background

People love to talk about themselves. So give them the chance. Ask questions about the listener's background in general, and include questions that will allow her to talk about her spiritual convictions as well.

- What was it like around your house growing up?
- What things were most important to your folks?
- Did you get in trouble a lot growing up?
- What did you get from your family that you want to pass on to your kids?
- How do you want to do things differently in your family?
- What are your brothers and sisters like? How are you alike/different?
- Did you grow up going to church? Did you enjoy it? (Or, if the person *didn't* grow up going to church: Do you wish you had?)
- Do you think you'll have your kids go to church someday?

2. *Questions Asking the Listener's Opinion or Advice*

I think the average listener is almost shocked to be asked for his or her opinion by someone who really wants to hear it. Endless topics and current events might encourage the listener to look at things from a spiritual perspective.

- I see you've got cable. What do you let your kids watch?
- What do you think of all the junk that's on the Internet? (I've yet to meet anyone who thinks it's *all* good.)
- Did you see *What Dreams May Come?* Incredible effects! What did you think about the way they pictured heaven?
- How do you celebrate Christmas at your house?
- What do you think about the cloning issue?
- Dr. Kevorkian is in the news again. What do you think of him?

3. *Questions that Involve the Listener's Imagination*

Some questions call on the listener to put himself in a certain situation and imagine what he'd do. This kind of "role-playing" can allow you to talk beyond the monotony of day-to-day events.

- Did you hear about Mary's diagnosis? What would you do if you found out *you* had cancer?
- If you had plenty of money and could do anything you want for a living, what would you do?
- What would you do if you found out *your* parents were planning to get a divorce?

4. *Questions that Ask for the Listener's Emotions*

On a daily basis, we rarely communicate beyond the factual level. A question that asks a listener to consider her feelings may cause her to see an issue in a completely different way.

- How do you feel about all these hate crimes?
- I have a friend whose husband has just been given three months to live. How would you feel if that were you?
- How would you feel if one of your kids really began to rebel?

- How would you feel if your house burned down and you lost everything?

I once asked a factory co-worker for his opinion about something in the Bible. I listened to his thoughts with very little comment. A week later he came back to me and said, "You know, I've been thinking about that question you asked me, and I think . . ." I've always wondered, if I had taken a different approach, if he would have come back and said, "You know, I've been thinking about that lecture you gave me . . ." By planting with good questions, a sower begins to encourage *two-way communication* on a spiritual level. Once that is accomplished, the harvest may be just around the corner.

Tool #2: Agreements

An old principle of persuasion says, "The first purpose of a persuasive speech is to show that not much persuasion is needed." In other words: A wise communicator seeks to build *agreements*, not *arguments*. *We're not that much different, you and I. We come from similar backgrounds. We want a lot of the same things out of life. We only differ at this one point.*

Many Christians attempt to communicate with unbelievers with a mind-set more like this: *We are completely different people, you and I. We are from different worlds. I am a citizen of the kingdom of heaven; you are from the domain of darkness. We think differently, we feel differently, we value different things.*

I've often marveled at the apostle Paul's approach to addressing unbelievers. In Acts 17, Paul had the opportunity to speak to a group of amateur philosophers on Mars Hill in Athens. In the days before cable, philosophy was the major sport of Athens, boasting of such past superstars as Socrates, Plato, and Aristotle. It was quite a spectator sport. "All the Athenians and the foreigners who lived there," the text says, "spent their time doing nothing but talking about and listening to the latest ideas" (v. 21 NIV). When the big day finally arrived for the Paul versus Athens showdown, a large group was gathered for the opening kickoff. Athens had the home field advantage.

It's hard to imagine two parties as different as Paul and the Athenians. Paul was Jewish; they were Greek or foreign. Paul was a

monotheist; they had statues of gods everywhere. Paul was committed to one Way, one Truth, and one Life; the Athenians constantly en-
tertained new ideas without committing to any of them. How
would *you* begin?

Paul had two choices. He could emphasize their *disagreements*—
of which there were many—or he could point out their *agreements.*
He wisely chose the latter. "Men of Athens," he began. "I see that in
every way you are very religious. For as I walked around and looked
carefully at your objects of worship, I even found an altar with this
inscription: TO AN UNKNOWN GOD. Now what you worship as
something unknown I am going to proclaim to you" (Acts 17:22–23
NIV). Eugene Peterson, in *The Message,* captures the tone of Paul's
words this way: "It is plain to see that you Athenians take your religion seriously. When I arrived here the other day, I was fascinated
with all the shrines I came across. And then I found one inscribed,
TO THE GOD NOBODY KNOWS. I'm here to introduce you to this
God so you can worship intelligently, know who you're dealing
with."

If you consider Paul's words carefully, you'll find that he used
three different techniques to build agreement with his audience.
First, he pointed out what they had in common. "Hey! We're both
into religion!" Second, he demonstrated knowledge of their world.
He pointed out that he had been in town for a while and he had tak-
en the time to view all of their "objects of worship"—notice that he
used a neutral term, and he made no comment or judgment about
these "objects" yet. Later on in the passage, Paul even went to the
trouble of quoting some of their own Greek poets, showing that he
had taken the time to understand their world before trying to
change it.

Finally, Paul suggested that not much persuasion is necessary.
Instead of commenting on the error of each shrine and idol, he simply pointed out one that had a blank label. All he wanted to do, he
seemed to say, was fill in that one little label. What could be more
painless?

Paul didn't have to begin that way. It would have been equally
accurate if he had chosen to stress his *disagreements* with the Athenians:
"O pagan philosophers and heathen Gentiles! Never have I seen
such idolatry and ignorance of the one true God. You even worship

unknown gods. Well, God is certainly not unknown to *me,* and I'm here to tell you all about Him." To summarize *this* approach: We are different, guess who's wrong, and you've got a lot of changing to do.

So why did Paul begin the way he did? I believe he chose to build agreements instead of arguments because his goal was not merely to *proclaim,* but to *persuade.* "And he was reasoning in the synagogue every Sabbath and trying to persuade Jews and Greeks" (Acts 18:4). Because their worlds were so different, there was very little chance that Paul could harvest that day, so he chose instead to sow. It worked. "We want to hear you again on this subject," some of them said. Eventually, "A few men became followers of Paul and believed" (Acts 17:32, 34 NIV).

The sower can apply Paul's principles today by seeking to build agreements instead of arguments with his listeners—but again, this is not easy for Christians. I said earlier that Christians, knowing that truth is on our side, tend to be *answer people*—and answer people find it hard to ask questions. In the same way, Christians have a very clear sense of exactly where we disagree with nonbelievers. As a result, we have a tendency to become *disagreement people* and to focus on the differences that exist between us instead of the common ground. Disagreement people find it difficult to find anything on which to agree. What do we really have in common?

That's the question the sower tries to answer, because the more agreement he can build with his listener, the smaller his persuasive task. As the sower encounters the friends, neighbors, and co-workers who inhabit or come across his turf each day, he can make a habit of reinforcing four messages in his listeners' minds that can greatly accelerate the harvest.

1. "We're Not So Different"

In Acts 22, Paul was surrounded in the temple by an angry mob. For his own protection, a group of Roman centurions arrested Paul and began to escort him to safety. But Paul asked permission of the commander to stop and address the crowd. Though Paul spoke to the Roman commander in Greek, he addressed the crowd in their *own* language—in Hebrew. "I am a Jew," he began, "born in Tarsus of Cilicia, but brought up in this city. Under Gamaliel I was thoroughly trained in the law of our fathers and was just as zealous for God as any of you are today" (Acts 22:3 NIV). As he spoke, we are told, the angry mob grew *quiet*. I believe the calming effect was the result of Paul's words: *I am one of you. We speak the same language. I grew up in this city. I went to school here. I was brought up like you, and I have many of the same values as you. We're not so different.* You can almost imagine the thoughts of the crowd: *Hey, he's one of us. How bad can he be?*

The sower can build agreement with his listener—and perhaps produce the same calming effect—by pointing out their common backgrounds. *I'm from the Midwest, too. Hey, that's where I went to college. I have three kids, too. Sure I like football. You know—we're not so different.* The nonbeliever needs to know that, though we believe in heaven and hell and God and angels and demons, we're not actually *from* Mars. He needs to know that our worlds overlap in some way and that we can still understand the world in which *he* lives and breathes.

2. "We Have Similar Values"

Every Christian knows that, in some ways, our standards are very different from the rest of the world. But Christians often fail to recognize that our standards and values are very similar in other ways—ways that can be pointed out to the listener. I've found that almost all parents, for example, desire to impart similar values to their children. I've never met a parent who hopes to raise *dis*honest and *dis*obedient kids. We may disagree on what obedience *looks* like, or how it is to be *instilled*—but the sower shouldn't overlook the fact that a common value may underlie our methodological differences. *We're trying to teach our kids to be responsible, too. How do you do it at your house?*

3. "We Have the Same Concerns and Interests"

C. S. Lewis once wrote, "The man who agrees with us that some important question, little regarded by others, is of great importance can be our Friend. He need not agree with us about the answer."[2] We disagree with non-Christians about all sorts of answers—but can we show them that we at least have a common concern about the questions? The statement, "I think the president's behavior was disgraceful" will draw a very different response than "I think the president should have been impeached." The opinion, "I think there's too much garbage on television" will draw almost universal agreement. The solution, "I think we need more censorship" will get much more varied responses.

I'm not suggesting that Christians revise all of their opinions to win the approval of non-Christian acquaintances. I'm simply saying that, though we commonly disagree with others on the specific solutions to problems, we shouldn't overlook the fact that we agree about the problems themselves. According to Lewis, that agreement alone may be enough to form a friendship. Agreements can be built when our listeners realize that we hold the same *concerns*. The discussion of *solutions* can be saved until the fruit has had a chance to ripen more.

4. "We Have the Same Needs"

Would you like to receive a hefty Christmas bonus this year? So would everyone else. Would you like to shed a few pounds and get back in shape? So would just about everyone else. In fact, many of your goals are so basic that they're shared by almost *all* people at your stage of life. Have you ever met a person who hopes to get sick, lose his house, and skip his vacation this year?

The man who walks up to a neighbor wearing his "To live is Christ" T-shirt may get a puzzled look; to the neighbor, to *live* is to eat, sleep, work, and play. The non-Christian suspects that belief in Christ is a call to abandon the material world and to think only of mystical, spiritual things. Far from it; the Christian faith is a call to *embrace* the world around us and to see all of life through a biblical worldview. The unbeliever's first chance to understand this is when we show her that we want many of the same things she does—but we may go about them in a very different way and for different reasons.

Tool #3: Your Life

As I said earlier, I've often marveled at the apostle Paul's approach to dealing with unbelievers. Acts 17 was one such example; in the book of 1 Thessalonians we see another. Paul had visited the Macedonian capital and had worked amidst great opposition to evangelize and found a church. Paul was finally forced to flee the city, but he was so concerned about the fate of the fledgling church he left behind that he sent Timothy back to strengthen and reassure them. Timothy brought back an encouraging report, which prompted Paul to write his first letter to the Thessalonians.

In that letter, Paul said something about his style of ministry to the Thessalonians. "As apostles of Christ we could have been a burden to you," he reminded them, "but we were gentle among you, like a mother caring for her little children. We loved you so much that we were delighted to share with you not only the gospel of God but our lives as well, because you had become so dear to us" (1 Thessalonians 2:6b–8 NIV).

Paul tells us that he planted far more than doctrinal truth in his listeners' lives; *he imparted his own life as well.* Thessalonica was a rough town for Christians, where opponents to the faith formed angry mobs and believers were dragged before city authorities. Paul knew that in that kind of environment, it would never be enough to simply ask good questions or build common ground. He had to get personally involved; his love, concern, and assurance of ongoing support would make all the difference for a Thessalonian counting the cost of belief in Christ.

In our country today no cities are quite as hostile to the faith as Thessalonica. Instead, in pockets *within* our cities—pockets sometimes as small as a family or marriage—faith in Christ is still met with Thessalonian rage. Paul's principle still applies; if we are hoping that people within these pockets will respond to Christ, we will need to plant our own lives as well.

I said earlier that the cost of faith in Christ is not the same for everyone, and that the sower must try to understand how much he is asking of his listener. It's one thing to be asked to jump from a burning building; it's another thing to be asked to jump when someone is offering to hold a safety net below. Both steps require courage, but not equal amounts of courage. Sometimes the unbeliever has a very clear concept of what he would leave behind by accepting Christ, but little idea of what awaits him when he jumps. "Are there people like *me* there? Is there anything to *do?* Does anybody have *fun?* I'm thinking of jumping—is anybody holding the net?"

The sower needs to be willing to say, "*I* will hold the net." Many writers have observed that one of the most important elements for an unbeliever considering conversion is his perceived sense of Christian community—or lack thereof. In other words, "I know the community I would leave behind; is any community waiting for me on the other side?" People in general have a powerful desire to *belong* and to be *accepted,* and these desires are not eliminated by faith in Christ. An unbeliever considering the gospel is not only asking, "Can I believe this?" but also, "Who would I *know* there? Would I *belong?*"

The sower's effort to plant not only with good questions and agreements but her own life as well may make all the difference in the future harvest. Three principles can help the sower impart her life in a genuine and effective way.

1. Be There for the Other Person's Agenda, Not Yours

In the second chapter of Job, Job's three friends made the decision to visit their grieving friend to "sympathize with him and comfort him. . . . Then they sat down on the ground with him for seven days and seven nights with no one speaking a word to him, for they saw that his pain was very great" (Job 2:11, 13). Originally, Job's counselors weren't counselors at all; they set off to see their friend with no agenda other than to be with him. The remarkable thing is that they considered this a worthwhile activity.

We live in a cynical age. When a stranger is unexpectedly friendly, the first thought that comes to mind is, *What does he want? Is he selling something, or does he want to sign me up for his multi-level marketing scheme?* In the busyness of modern life, we often seek out others only when we *want* something from them. Unfortunately, Christians are sometimes guilty of the same fault. What comes to our neighbor's mind when our *first sign* of friendliness is followed by an evangelistic presentation?

Christians are quick to say, "But I don't want anything *from* my neighbor. I have something *for* my neighbor—the gift of salvation." But does that ring any truer to the neighbor than when a salesman comes to his front door and begins, "Now, I'm not here to *sell* you anything"? Of course he is there to sell something, and of course the Christian wants something from his neighbor: his time, his attention, and, hopefully, his commitment.

A wise sower begins to sow his life in the lives of those around him long before he wants anything in return. Like Job's friends, the sower understands that there is a time just to "sympathize and comfort," asking nothing in return. Our willingness to serve our neighbor's agenda now might determine whether he is ever willing to consider ours later.

2. Take Him, Don't Send Him

Why say to a neighbor, "You really ought to go to church," when you can say, "Why don't you come to church with me?" Why say, "That's a movie you really ought to see," when you can say, "I'm going to rent that video Friday night. Why don't you come over?" The obvious reason we often say the former instead of the latter is that it takes much less time to *send* someone than to *take* him yourself. But advice is cheap. I'm willing to recommend any number of things that cost me nothing and bring me no risk of failure. "Have you invested in this mutual fund? *You* really should."

In a busy world, the extent to which we're willing to invest our own life tells a person a lot about how much we really care—and a lot about the reality of the gospel. Paul thought it wise to invest in the Thessalonians in this way; his relationship with them may have been the critical support that helped them to continue to believe in the midst of a hostile environment.

3. Be There After the Deal Is Signed

A current series of radio commercials for an automobile insurance company stresses the importance of having a *local* company. *Sure*, they say, *anybody* can sell you an insurance policy; but what happens when you have a question? How fast will they get there if you have an accident? *Where will they be when you need them?* That question is an important one for every harvester. Sometimes, in our desire to see people come to Christ, we see the moment of conversion as a kind of finish line, like graduation from college. Instead, we need to see conversion as it is biblically described—as a kind of birth. A new life has begun, but it's a very fragile and dependent life that needs our ongoing love and care—and the broader love and care of a church family. The sower needs to make it clear by word *and* deed that her relationship with the listener is not a security blanket that will be pulled away once the baby is born.

Harvesters may argue that this principle of "planting your own life" simply takes us back to the old question of friendship evange-lism. "Is it really necessary to build a relationship with everyone you meet before you can say anything about the gospel?" No, but the concept of sowing recognizes that there are different kinds of fruit and that fields ripen at an uneven rate. Some personalities are more individualistic and are much less concerned about community. But others care very much, and a developing relationship with that kind of person can make all the difference. The sower must determine the type of fruit before he decides the method of harvest. One thing he knows for certain—one technique does not fit all.

Every day, with everyone he meets, the sower attempts to culti-vate the soil and plant the seed. The three planting tools we've looked at in this chapter—questions, agreements, and your own life —all involve the sower himself. But there is something else the sow-er can use to plant, something external to himself: He can expose the unbeliever to a wide variety of books, tapes, movies, and other mate-rials that help the sower to easily and naturally interact with the un-believer about spiritual topics. But as we'll see in the next chapter, not just any materials will do.

Chapter 11 | # PLANTING PART 2— MATERIALS

I remember visiting a Christian bookstore once—I use the word *bookstore* loosely, because in reality more than half the store was devoted to music, posters, and an astounding variety of what I call "Protestant Paraphernalia." I was amazed to find an entire section devoted to T-shirts, lapel pins, and bumper stickers. One stylish crew neck featured a drawing of a plump pink human brain with the caption, "This is your brain." Below it was a drawing of the same brain sitting in a frying pan. The caption: "This is your brain in hell." A jet-black Beefy-T featured the subtle invitation, "Heaven or hell, turn or burn." Still another was emblazoned with the warm reassurance, "Every knee shall bow—count on it." Every pin, shirt, poster, and sticker was a stark, screaming, in-your-face confrontation with the unbelieving world. "This is how it *is*," they all seemed to say. "Like it or lump it, baby." Above this remarkable display was a banner that read, "Witness Center." Until I saw that banner it had not occurred to me that these pins, shirts, and bumper stickers were much more than some Christian's concept of art—they represented some Christian's concept of the *best way to witness to an unbeliever.*

I have a brother-in-law who is a senior vice president for a large advertising agency in Chicago. I asked him once how an especially obnoxious television commercial for a local car dealer managed to stay on the air. "What's the name of the dealer?" he asked. When I told him, he replied, "*That's* why it stays on the air. You remember the *name.*" In advertising, the assumption is made that people are busy, distracted, and essentially immune to the thousands of messages that bombard them each day. If an advertisement can just shout loud enough, just assault the senses long enough, then the message might get through. Christians often work under the same assumption. If we can catch the unbeliever's eye, if we can make him pay attention for a moment, the message just might get through.

What message? When a man is slapped in the face, it's only in commercials that he responds with, "Thanks. I needed that." In the real world, he's very likely to slap you back. Christians everywhere walk around adorned with slogans and clichés that appear blunt, angry, self-righteous, and confrontational to the average unbeliever. The message gets through—the message that Christians are rude, arrogant, and judgmental. "Heaven or hell, turn or burn" doesn't shock *me*—but then, I've already turned. The question is, what kind of T-shirt do you wear around someone who's still deciding whether or not to follow Christ?

This issue is a critical one for the sower, and the problem is not restricted to Christian T-shirts and bumper stickers. It's also a problem with Christian books, magazines, television shows, and movies. The sower knows that books, tapes, and other materials could be very helpful in the ongoing process of sowing. She'd love to give a book to a friend, leave a tape with a co-worker, or encourage a neighbor to see a movie, all in the hopes of planting a few seeds of biblical worldview. But *what* book, tape, or movie?

Five Criteria for a Good Sowing Tool

I have a Christian friend, a former pastor, who now works for a financial investment firm in Austin. On his desk he keeps a stack of books—just four books—that he considers "safe" to give to a genuine non-Christian. It's a sobering thought that, of the thousands of Christian titles currently in print, my friend can find only four that he considers safe for a sower to recommend.[1]

I asked my friend what he means by a "safe" book. He said that to recommend a Christian book in the workplace is to put himself at risk; he wants to be sure that the recipient isn't insulted or offended by the experience. To safeguard against this risk, the careful sower should look at five criteria before recommending a book or *any* material to an unbeliever.

1. The Materials Must Speak the Unbeliever's Language

Our planet has hundreds of distinct languages, each incomprehensible to the person who lives just across the border. Nothing is as frustrating as trying to communicate with someone who has no vocabulary in common with us. "Those French people!" Steve Martin once complained, "It's like they have a different word for everything!" To the ancient Greeks, foreigners sounded like they were just mumbling nonsense—something like "barbarbarbarbar." That's the origin of the word *barbarian*. The modern definition of the word is "an insensitive, uncultured person; a boor." Originally, it simply meant "someone who doesn't speak your language." I imagine it was a small step from the first definition to the second.

One of the unique languages of our planet is Christianese. It's really a blending of several other dialects, including ancient Greek and Hebrew, King James English, and pop psychobabble. Here is just a brief excerpt from the elementary Christianese lexicon.

- Saved
- Justified
- Sanctified
- Glorified
- Heathen

- Witness
- Gospel
- Spirit-filled
- Raptured

This is *basic* vocabulary, of course. The advanced lexicon includes terms like *premillennial* and *dispensationalist*. We even have Christianese secret codes to learn, like 666 and WWJD.

This is the Christian's native tongue. But how does it sound to the unbeliever when we attempt to communicate to *him* in this mysterious language? We sound like barbarians in the fully modern sense of the word. Because we don't take the time to speak and write in a way the non-Christian can understand, we appear as insensitive and uncultured boors. Those *Christians*—it's like they have a different word for *everything*.

As Christians we are essentially *translators*. Our job is to take complex theological principles, first recorded in ancient Near Eastern texts, and express them in terms so simple and clear that the most uneducated modern listener can understand them. Translation takes *time*, and it requires the knowledge of at least two languages: the language of your original text and the language of your listener. A truly effective translation is faithful to *both*.

Any book, tape, or magazine intended for a nonbeliever needs to speak in the language of the unbeliever. It should not require knowledge of the Bible or church culture to understand it. This does not mean that Christian concepts must always be dumbed down— "sin" should not have to be repackaged as "dysfunction," for example—but it should be free of unnecessary jargon and clichés that might sound confusing or offensive to "pagans." And it should do all this without talking down to the unbeliever in a simplistic or condescending way.

2. The Materials Must Show an Understanding of the Unbeliever's World

I have a friend who is in graduate school at a state university. In his department, the belief that homosexuality is the moral equivalent of heterosexuality is so entrenched that it is absolutely non-negotiable. As he puts it, "In my department, to argue that homosexuality is a sin would be no different than to argue that blacks are really inferior to whites." Knowledge of this mind-set is very helpful to my friend—and an ignorance of that mind-set would be disastrous for any Christian who assumed otherwise. Fifty years ago a Christian could assume that an unbeliever held many similar attitudes and viewpoints about life, ethics, and morality. In the day in which we live, the unbeliever's world can be radically different from our own. Instead of attempting to persuade unbelievers about details of biblical morality—which should be the result of salvation, not a prerequisite for it—a wise sower takes the time to find out exactly how our worlds are different before charging ahead.

James Davison Hunter, in his book *Culture Wars,* wrote that communities that share firmly held beliefs—like Christians—need to try to understand what *other* communities hold dear. We need to try to recognize "the 'sacred' within different moral communities. The 'sacred' is that which communities love and revere as nothing else. The 'sacred' expresses that which is non-negotiable and defines the limits of what they will tolerate."[2] In other words, Christians are not the only ones who hold things sacred, and an affront to the deeply held beliefs of others—whether about homosexuality, feminism, or radical environmentalism—is seen by them as not just offensive, but *sacrilegious.* We do not have to agree with another person's point of view in order to respect that person and avoid obvious offense. Hunter warns us not to be "idiots," which comes from the Greek prefix *idios,* meaning personal, private, or separate. A true idiot, in the original sense of the word, was a person so private and withdrawn that he had no idea how to speak or act.

What is your listener's religious and cultural background? What community does she consider herself a part of? What stereotypes or caricatures would she find particularly offensive? What agreements have you assumed between you and your listener that may actually be points of difference? The sower can avoid the particular form of idiocy common to Christians if she will take the time to understand her listener's world—and make sure that any material she recommends does the same.

3. The Materials Must Be Intelligent and Credible

In public restrooms I have sometimes found Christian tracts that believers have left—not simple summaries of the gospel like *The Roman Road* or *The Bridge,* but tracts that attempt to deal with a complex contemporary issue such as evolution, feminism, homosexuality, or AIDS. In one tract on evolution, Darwin's basic theory was portrayed in such simplistic terms that no evolutionist on earth would recognize it. The theory was then neatly "refuted," and the Christians won in the end. This kind of argument is known as a "straw man." We set up a straw man—a flimsy facsimile of a real argument—and then we knock it down. This is a common in-house exercise for Christians, and it gives us a temporary sense of confidence and superiority; but God help you if you ever run into the *real* argument.

My son will enter college soon—probably a large, secular university. There, for the first time, he will encounter some of the *real* arguments. It will be a vulnerable time for him. Many young Christians abandon their faith during their college years, for a variety of reasons. One of those reasons is that they were never prepared to resist an effective argument made by a knowledgeable, intelligent, persuasive professor. When the genuine item comes along, the young Christian is swept away. He may end up angry and bitter, feeling that he was misinformed, misled, or even deceived by his Christian mentors.

Sometimes we unintentionally cheat younger Christians by exposing them only to imitations of challenges to the Christian faith, versions that are easy to defeat because they bear little resemblance to the real disease. My wife and I are working now to try to "inoculate" our son against those arguments. When a doctor inoculates a patient, he injects a weakened form of a disease into the patient's body. The patient's immune system detects the new disease and begins to develop antibodies to resist it. By the time the *real* disease comes along, the patient has sufficient immunity to resist it. But here's the key: *The inoculation must contain a sample of the real disease.*

One of the ways we hope to prepare our son to face the real arguments is by admitting honestly that the other side is not *stupid.* We simply believe they are *mistaken,* and sometimes very intelligent people make mistakes. By refusing to ridicule or caricature opposing views, we hope to teach our son to approach opponents with *respect.* As Peter put it, "Always be prepared to give an answer to everyone who asks you to give the reason for the hope that you have. But do this with gentleness and respect" (1 Peter 3:15b NIV).

The materials that sowers give to unbelievers must address them as intelligent, thoughtful adults, and should deal with their positions gently and respectfully. This means that Christian speakers and authors who want to create materials that a sower can recommend had better do their homework. They need to take the time to intimately understand an opposing view from *original* sources—in other words, they need to have the courage to expose themselves to the real disease in its most virulent form. Then, they need to formulate intelligent and well-thought-out responses. Even if the unbeliever disagrees, as long as he feels that his position was handled fairly and respectfully, he'll remain open to further input from the sower.

4. The Materials Must Raise Good Questions

I used to write a syndicated comic strip called "Downstown" for Universal Press Syndicate. My strip dealt with the lives of singles and their relationships, sometimes drawing on biblical themes. I once published a collection of my work, and I thought I'd drop by a local Christian bookstore to see if they might want to carry it. The manager flipped through the book, then looked up at me suspiciously. "Is this a *Christian* book?" she asked.

I had no idea what to say. What exactly *is* a Christian book? As I recall, my answer was, "Well . . . I'm a Christian, and I wrote it." I don't think that's what she had in mind. She meant, "Is this book blatantly and openly about Christian things?" As it turns out, I had written a non-Christian book.

Think of the term "Christian movie." What does it suggest to you? How would you characterize it? Sometimes after seeing a movie we will report to one another, "It was really good, but it wasn't exactly a *Christian* film." What we mean is either that the movie violated some biblical norm—there was profanity or illicit sexuality—or that the movie wasn't blatantly and openly about Christian things. There was no mention of God or Jesus or heaven or hell. There were a lot of good *questions,* but no clear *answers.* As I said before, Christians are answer people, and a film that gives no answers can hardly be called *Christian.* We reserve the term "Christian movie" for Billy Graham films and the evangelistic videos we use in our youth groups—films that give *answers.*

In this book I've tried to draw a contrast between the activities of sowing and harvesting; we also need to consider the difference between the books, tapes, and films that are suited for sowing, and those that are better for harvesting. Harvesting materials do what the harvester does—they give answers. They are up-front, direct, and thorough. Although they may address a topic other than the gospel, they will always come around to the topic of the gospel itself, and they usually attempt to bring the unbeliever to a point of decision. For the harvester, if the book or movie doesn't give the whole answer, it's of no value.

Sowing materials, on the other hand, do what the sower does; they ask *questions*. For the sower, any book, tape, or film that raises questions that the sower can make use of in his ongoing contact with the unbeliever is of *great* value. That's one of the biggest differences between a harvesting and sowing tool: A harvesting tool does all the work for you. "Here—read this and become a Christian." But a sowing tool still leaves the sower with most of the work. "Here—read this and tell me what you think." All a sower's movie does is raise a good question, create a deeper interest, or provide an opening for an intimate conversation.

This is the radical claim I am putting forth: *Because sowing is a legitimate, God-ordained form of ministry, materials that help us sow are valuable ministry tools—if only we will learn how to recognize and use them.*

In 1981, when the movie *Chariots of Fire* was released, there was great celebration in the evangelical community. At last! Hollywood had released a Christian film—almost. Many Christians—many *harvesters*—were disappointed in the film. Sure, it cast a conservative Christian in a positive light and sure, it had occasional references to Scripture and missions—but if only we could add a gospel presentation to the end of the movie, *then* we would have something.

The problem the harvester faces is that very few true harvesting movies exist, and mainstream Hollywood will *never* release one. Harvesting movies just can't compete with the production values of a big-budget film. The result is that our harvesting materials often look second-rate, amateurish, and out-of-date. And how do you recommend one to a genuine non-Christian? "Hey, have you seen *The Mark of the Beast?* You can rent it at the Christian bookstore." Sadly, the harvester's toolbox is often a meager collection of well-worn tools.

The wonderful thing about sowing tools is that the secular world is making them *for* us. Chuck Colson once said that he learned more about the true nature of sin by watching Woody Allen's movie *Crimes and Misdemeanors* than from any doctrinal treatise he ever read. The movie is about an eminent ophthalmologist, a well-respected family man, who has a brief affair with a lonely flight attendant. The flight attendant becomes increasingly jealous and threatens to reveal the affair to the doctor's wife. In a panic, the doctor turns to his brother, who has Mafia connections. The brother suggests that he can "take care of things," and he arranges to have her murdered. The rest of the movie is about the doctor's attempt to rationalize his terrible sin in his own mind. He tells himself that the woman was an enemy, threatening to destroy his marriage, his family, and his reputation. What choice did he have but to defend himself? By the end of the film, he has fully rationalized his sin, and he lives happily ever after.

The title, *Crimes and Misdemeanors,* is a takeoff on Dostoyevsky's famous novel *Crime and Punishment.* In the novel, a student commits a murder to test his right to transgress moral law. He is so tormented by guilt and remorse that he finally confesses. His crime was followed by punishment; in Allen's film, the doctor's crime was never confessed *or* punished. Allen was saying that people have a tremendous capacity to rationalize away their sinfulness and to think of their crimes as simple misdemeanors.[3]

Imagine that a sower and his neighbor both see this film. Afterward, some very natural interaction about the movie might include comments like these:

- Can you believe the way the doctor rationalized what he did?
- How do you feel about the fact that he got away with it in the end?
- Do you think he *really* got away with it?
- Do you suppose he would ever again think about what he did?
- What do you think Woody Allen was saying about human nature?

Simple questions like these could lead to some *very* direct conversation about biblical topics like sin, confession, and repentance. As the sower grows in skill and experience, she realizes that she can make use of an incredible variety of books, tapes, music, and films that can be found at *any* bookstore or video outlet. Instead of trying to figure out how to get the unbeliever to come over to *my* world and watch *my* movie, I can learn to make use of the movies from *his* world that he's most likely to see.

The sower must be on the constant lookout for books, tapes,

films, and any other material that could open a door to the spiritual dimension of life. As Pascal observed, people are spiritually uninterested because they are *distracted*—but a big part of modern distraction is the endless flood of magazines, novels, movies, and TV shows that vie for our attention. If Christians can learn to use those materials, we can learn to inject spiritual topics into daily life in a natural and unassuming way.

5. The Materials Must Have a Reasonable Persuasive Goal

John Warwick Montgomery tells the story of an eager Christian who was witnessing to his scientifically minded friend. Their conversation was stalled over the issue of evolution; according to the unbeliever, there simply isn't enough evidence in the geologic record to support the biblical account of creation. Undaunted, the Christian replied, "Now what was that book I heard about that refutes all of geology?"

Some Christians believe that such a book is possible. They fail to understand that modern geology, and virtually every other academic discipline, is supported by a mammoth amount of study, research, and writing. Any attempt to refute in one swoop such a massive amount of scholarship displays ignorance of the field and loses credibility in the eyes of the unbeliever. "You must be kidding —*it's not that simple.*"

That's why it's important for Christians not to bite off more than they can chew when appealing to unbelievers. I once heard a tape by a Christian with a Ph.D. in chemistry. He was examining the big bang theory of the origin of the universe, questioning whether such an event could have happened without some external guidance. He was an active scientist with a credible degree from a respected university, and his arguments were impressive—his only problem was the extent of his persuasive goal. In a one-hour tape he went from flaws in the big bang theory to the biblical account of creation to the New Testament teaching that "in Him all things hold together." The farther he went, the more his argument seemed to unravel; it was just too much to cover in an hour.

One exciting application of the principle of "small bites" is the number of respected scientists who are now writing on design theory. To put it simply, design theory is creation science with a more reasonable persuasive goal. Design theorists argue that, when you consider the existence and nature of the universe, it seems as though *some* kind of intelligent design was necessary to produce it. They are not arguing that it must have been the biblical God, or that the Genesis account of creation must be true. They are arguing *one small point* —but *that* small point is enough to upend the theory of evolution.

These scientists have realized that within the scientific community, they would be deadlocked *forever* debating the larger issue of "creation science" and whether it even *exists*. There is no way to move their colleagues from the position of scientific naturalism all the way to Christian theism in a single step—so they have decided to sow. Their more limited persuasive goal is much more attainable, and the writings they're producing are intelligent, credible, and persuasive—exactly what the sower is looking for.

Using Good Sowing Materials

If you consider carefully the five criteria of good sowing materials I've described above, you understand why my friend in Austin was only able to find four "safe" books to give away to his unbelieving friends. But why is this the case? *Thousands* of Christian titles are currently in print. Why are there so few materials produced for the sower?

One of the reasons, as I've said throughout this book, is that sowing is rarely viewed as a significant form of ministry. Why create materials to do what has so little value? An equally valid reason is that sowing materials fall into a publishing "dead zone." Christians buy books written *by* Christians *for* Christians; what Christian wants to buy a book written *by* a Christian but *for* a nonbeliever? This kind of book might seem watered-down or evasive to the Christian. Where are the Scripture citations? Why is the author taking so long to get to the point? This message doesn't *preach*.

Who wants a book like that? A sower does—but at this time in church history, sowers are in short supply. Until the number of active sowers increases—until a new *market* is created—good sowing materials will continue to be in short supply. The best sowing books seem to have been written by really savvy Christians of past decades: Walker Percy, Dorothy Sayers, C. S. Lewis, G. K. Chesterton, etc. We could use more contemporary writers like them! For now, the best sowing books, tapes, and movies are produced by the secular world. All the sower needs to do is learn to recognize them—and we can recognize them using the five criteria of this chapter:

- It must speak the unbeliever's language.
- It must show an understanding of the unbeliever's world.
- It must be intelligent and credible.
- It must raise good questions.
- It must have a reasonable persuasive goal.

Once the sower has cultivated the soil and planted, his only remaining job before harvest is to nurture: to do whatever he can, day after day, to make sure that what he has planted takes root and grows.

Chapter 12 | NURTURING

Every year, growing up in the suburbs of St. Louis, my family planted a garden. Gardening had nothing to do with need; food was no farther away than the local A & P. Gardening was a kind of suburban ritual, a chance to feel like we were making good use of the land, a guilt offering for building too many golf courses. The goal, by summer's end, was to be able to grace the doorsteps of our neighbors with bountiful bags of zucchini and other inedible vegetables.

Every year, we set aside two rows in our garden for radishes— "Cherry Belle" radishes as the Burpee Company called them. I can still picture the image on the seed package of bulging scarlet orbs the size of baseballs. I've often wondered if that photo was doctored— enlarged to show texture, perhaps. Based on the results of *our* garden, I believe that an actual radish is about the size of a Tic Tac.

To be fair, the problem was not the Burpee Seed Company. The problem was me. When radishes begin to mature below ground they put out bushy green leaves above. Unfortunately, there's no way to tell by the size of the leaves how big the radish is below. I assumed the leaves were like the pop-up thermometer on the Thanksgiving turkey: When the leaves are up, the radish is done. Time after time I eagerly pulled up a fistful of thick green leaves only to find a tiny pink BB below. Unfortunately, once a radish is uprooted it can't be replanted. That's the end of it, and all you have to take in for dinner is a handful of leaves.

Instead of hurrying to harvest, I should have spent my time making sure each radish had an unhindered opportunity to grow. If you think about it for a moment, that's all a gardener really does. A gardener has no power to make things grow; he is simply an *environmentalist*. His job is to create the optimum environment for growth to take place. After that, the radish is on its own.

The same is true for the sower. The fate of the unbeliever is ultimately out of the sower's control, regardless of his cultivating and planting skills. But the sower needs to remember that, once the cultivating and planting are done, there is still work that he can do. He can be an environmentalist who helps to maintain an atmosphere where the seed that he has planted can take root and grow. In other words, he can nurture the soil.

Jesus told us in the parable of the sower that seed can be destroyed well *after* the planting process, as in the case of the seed that is choked out by thorns. The soil was good, the seed was good, but the plants were unable to compete over time with the thorns. What happens if the sower pulls a few weeds?

There are three tasks the sower can perform on an ongoing basis to help nurture and encourage the growth of his friends and neighbors toward an eventual harvest. Those tasks are watering the garden, pruning and caring for the vine, and tending the soil.

Watering the Garden

The ultimate fate of the unbeliever is outside the sower's hands. This principle is much more than a cursory tip of the hat in God's direction; the danger of this book is that it might lead an enthusiastic sower to believe that he can produce a harvest through his own cleverness and skill. Not so. Conversion is first, last, and always an act of God. "No one knows the Son except the Father," Jesus reminded us, "nor does anyone know the Father except the Son, and anyone to whom the Son wills to reveal him" (Matthew 11:27b). But God invites us to take an active part in His process of conversion, not only through the work of sowing and harvesting, but through prayer.

I've chosen the term "Watering the Garden" to represent this process simply because water is often used in the Bible to represent the Holy Spirit and His work. "'Whoever believes in me, as the Scripture has said, streams of living water will flow from within him.' By this he meant the Spirit" (John 7:38–39a NIV). To "water the garden," then, is simply to invite the Spirit to do what only He can—draw men to God through Christ.

The sower needs to see prayer as an integral part of the sowing process. It's one thing to recognize a soil deficiency like prejudice, but to amend that deficiency requires a change of the human heart. It's one thing to recommend a book that deals with a spiritual topic, but to spark a genuine spiritual hunger requires a work of the Spirit. Think through the people you identified as a part of your turf. Knowing what you know of the condition of their soil, what is the most significant thing you can pray for each one right now?

Water is essential to all life on our planet. The farmer can do his work with great cleverness and skill, but if he forgets to water, there will be no life. The same principle applies to the sower. In our enthusiasm for our work, we must never forget that, apart from Him, we can do nothing.

Pruning and Caring for the Vine

I learned about pruning by watching my father grow tomatoes. My father *loved* tomatoes, and any true gardener will understand what I mean when I say that he loved to *grow* them far more than he loved to *eat* them. In the summers, every day after work my father would mount his sixteen-horsepower Bolens tractor to drive the exhausting hundred feet to the end of our house where the tomato plants resided. The tractor pulled a wagon loaded with a formidable array of tomato-growing tools, chemicals, and accessories. He had twist ties and cloth strips for tying up vines; blossom-set sprays to keep tomato blossoms from prematurely falling from the vine; exotic fertilizers and supplements in a variety of colors and forms; and even a little postage scale to weigh each finished product.

Watching my father wade into the tomato plants was very much like watching a beekeeper tending his hives. Dad was fully "suited up" for the occasion, and he entered his garden prepared to do a variety of jobs. If you looked over his garden after he had finished, you could see his handprints everywhere: A vine was bound up here, an extra long stake was added there, a puff of pesticide powder had been put on this plant, and a pile of discarded weeds lay beside another. Dad's goal was to do whatever was necessary every day to give each plant its best opportunity to bear fruit.

The sower's goal is the same. In the process of caring for the vine, there are two essential tasks the sower can perform.

1. The sower can watch for bugs and parasites.

In farming, the greatest dangers are often the smallest. In the parable of the sower, the seed was destroyed by birds, rocks, and thorns, not by earthquakes and floods. Farmers sweat the small stuff, like aphids, corn blight, and boll weevils. Some pests that can bring a crop to ruin are too small to see with the naked eye.

For the sower, bugs and parasites are the periodic distractions that can bring the unbeliever's spiritual interest to a standstill. Several years ago, I knew a man who worked out at the same gym that I did. We had spoken a few times, but one day he seemed especially cold. I was wearing a T-shirt that said, "Fight the good fight of faith." He frowned and asked, "That's a little antagonistic, don't you think?" To him, my shirt suggested Crusaders massacring Turkish peasants, not an internal struggle to maintain a fervent belief. My T-shirt was a parasite that leeched the life from his spiritual interest; until I had the chance to spray that particular bug, my sowing had come to a halt.

A parasite could be as simple as an article in the newspaper or a segment on the evening news: The Jesus Seminar reports that only 10 percent of the words attributed to Jesus in the New Testament were actually said by Him; a famous pastor confesses to embezzling millions in ministry funds; archaeologists report that no trace of the Exodus has ever been found. These things seem so *small,* so irrelevant to the real gospel—small and irrelevant to *us,* that is. To the unbeliever they are parasites, apparently minor infestations that, left unchecked, can eventually destroy the entire plant.

A parasite could be a personal or professional problem that, like the thorns in the parable, threaten to choke the life from the unbeliever's interest. Sometimes in our zeal for ministry we try to ignore the personal problems of our listeners; unfortunately, those very problems are sometimes so great a distraction that they prevent the unbeliever from giving attention to the gospel.

A parasite could be any one of a thousand things: a negative comment from a spouse or friend, a visit from a representative of another religion, even a doubt or fear that seems to come out of thin air. In each case, the sower must try to identify the pest and deal with it in an appropriate way. A note of encouragement, an article in rebuttal, an answer to a perplexing question, or even a simple conversation can be enough to stop a potential infestation in its tracks.

2. The sower can look for suckers.

On a tomato plant, there is a special kind of shoot that starts to grow from the exact intersection of two other shoots. It's called a "sucker." A sucker looks very much like any other shoot; in fact, if you let it grow long enough, it's virtually indistinguishable. The only problem is that suckers drain a great deal of energy from the plant— *and they don't bear fruit.*

Suckers represent the dozens of issues, tangents, and diversions that could sidetrack the sower from the central issue of the gospel. As I said before, Christians tend to be answer people, and the problem isn't simply that we have answers, but that we have *too many* answers. Search Ministries is an organization that deals with this problem all the time. Search's central ministry function is known as an Open Forum. A core group of Christians is asked to invite non-Christian friends and neighbors to an open-ended discussion where they will feel comfortable and free to give their opinions about general spiritual topics. The goal is to create an atmosphere where the unbeliever feels welcome and respected. Over a process of weeks, as the unbeliever feels that he has been heard, he becomes more open to spiritual input in return.

The most difficult part of this process is the Christians. The first step in an Open Forum is to impress the host Christians that ultimate success depends, to put it bluntly, on their ability to keep their mouths shut. You can imagine that in a genuinely open-ended discussion among unbelievers, some remarkably unbiblical opinions can be aired. The Christian's instinct is to pounce on each error like a tiger on its prey. But a tiger only gets to pounce once; if he jumps too soon, the prey is off and running.

Abraham Lincoln, when he was a trial lawyer in Illinois, once said, "I am willing to concede every point to my opponent—*except the most important one.*" Christians are often unwilling to concede *any* point at all. Aware that Truth is on our side, we consider *every* error an assault to be repelled. As a result, we often wander off on a hundred rabbit trails instead of staying on the road we hoped would lead to the gospel. We end up not only trying to convince the non-Christian about salvation by grace, but also about euthanasia, smoking, dancing, and welfare spending.

Lincoln's policy showed an exceptional wisdom and self-discipline, a keen grasp of what C. S. Lewis called a "sense of the center." Lewis urged Christians to think carefully about *the most important issue* and to try very hard not to be distracted from it. When the sower gives in to the temptation to argue a non-essential topic with the unbeliever, a sucker results. A vine begins to grow that may draw more and more energy away from the plant, but it will never bear fruit. Even if the sower finally convinces the unbeliever to quit smoking—is *that* what he was after?

The key to recognizing a sucker is knowing the true vine. The sucker is always an *offshoot.* That's why Lewis encouraged Christians to focus on *mere Christianity.* The questions every sower must ask are, "What *is* the basic gospel? What are the *essential* issues? What points can I concede to the unbeliever (or at least ignore), and what points constitute a challenge to the gospel itself?"

Tending the Soil

In North Carolina where I live, only a couple of varieties of grass seem to thrive. Most lawns are planted with fescue, a thick, coarse grass that does well under summer drought and children's feet, the two chief nemeses of lawns everywhere. Unfortunately, fescue doesn't reseed itself. Every fall busy homeowners line the rental stores, signing up for aerators, dethatchers, and slit seeders, beginning the annual ritual of the replanting of the lawn. To put it another way: Lawns in North Carolina stay lush and green only because they remain in a constant state of planting.

In chapters 10 and 11 I described the process of planting in an unbeliever's life. The sower can use the tools of questions, agreements, his own life, and a wide variety of helpful materials to begin to introduce the subject of spiritual things into an unbeliever's life. But the mistake would be to think of planting as a one-time event: Here's a good book; I've done my job. Like the homeowner of North Carolina, the sower needs to think of planting as a continual, ongoing process.

What does this ongoing process look like? To try to put the sower's ongoing job in simple, practical terms, let's try to visualize a sower's day. Let's imagine a fictional sower named John, who encounters his first fellow human being of the day as he picks up his morning paper at the end of the driveway. John speaks first, or there probably would be no communication.

John:	Hey neighbor!
Jim:	Man, I hate getting up when it's still dark.
John:	Can you believe it? God goes to all the trouble of designing a universe where the sun comes up every morning and what do we do? We invent alarm clocks to get up while it's dark!
Jim:	Ain't it the truth.

At breakfast, John scans the morning paper. He makes a mental note of two articles that he can use later in the day. He takes a few minutes to pray before he leaves for work. He prays for his wife and his kids, and he remembers to pray for his next-door neighbor, whom he has invited to church on Sunday. There is a honk as John's car pool arrives. They talk on the way to work.

Margaret:	Did anybody catch *Jerry Springer* last night? They did a piece on "remarried men telling their wives that their divorce was never finalized."
John:	I know people who *love* that show and people who *hate* that show. What do you think, Margaret?
Margaret:	I think people make a big deal out of nothing. Most of it is just staged, anyway. It's no different than professional wrestling.
Joe Bob:	Now, hold on there.

John: What would you do if you found out *your* husband
            was still married to someone else?

Margaret: I think I'd kill myself. Or I'd kill him. I don't know
            what I'd do.

John: I think what we could use is a rulebook for marriage.

Margaret: You can say that again.

Joe Bob: Are you saying wrestling is *fake?*

            At work, John is doing performance reviews, and he is mak-
            ing some suggestions for improving an employee's perfor-
            mance. Last month John recommended that she read First
            Things First *by Stephen Covey, which the employee great-*
            ly enjoyed.

Maria: I think that book changed my life. Stephen Covey
            must be a genius to come up with that *First Things*
            First.

John: He didn't come up with it. Would you like to see
            someone else who wrote about the same thing be-
            fore him? *(John takes a book from his shelf.)* Listen to
            this: "Put first things first and we get second things
            thrown in: put second things first and we lose both
            first and second things."

Maria: That's great! Who wrote that?

John: A guy named C. S. Lewis wrote it over fifty years ago.
            It's from an essay he wrote called "First and Second
            Things." Here, you can borrow it. If you like it, I've
            got some other books by Lewis that you'll like even
            more.

            During the day, John takes a minute to drop in on a friend
            whose wife is in the hospital.

John: I saw an article in the paper this morning that made
            me think of you. Some studies have shown that pa-
            tients who are prayed for actually recover faster than
            those who are not.

Eddie: Sounds great. Do you know anybody who prays? *(He*
            laughs.)

John: *(He laughs too.)* I do. Personally, Eddie, I don't think
            prayer heals people; I think God does—and He lis-
            tens to prayers. I just wanted you to know that Mary

and I are praying for your wife every evening before bedtime.

Eddie: *(After a long pause)* Thanks. I appreciate that.

At lunch, John sits with a friend who, like John, coaches his son's soccer team.

John: How do you deal with a kid who has no respect for authority?

George: I've got a couple of kids like that.

John: It seems to me that I'm doing a lot more than coaching soccer; I'm trying to impart some basic values to the kids.

George: I never thought about it that way.

John: What sort of values do you want to build into *your* team?

George: Well, let's see . . . I suppose teamwork and self-control . . . maybe drive and determination . . .

John: Good ideas. I never knew soccer was such a spiritual game.

That afternoon, John drops by the office of a co-worker.

John: I've noticed from some of the decorations in your office that you're Muslim. I'd love to learn more about the Muslim faith. Can you give me anything to read?

Kajik: Oh yes, I could do that. *(He reaches for a book on his shelf.)*

John: I'm very interested in spiritual things, and I thought you'd be a good source. Would you mind if I had some questions for you after I read this?

Kajik: Perhaps we could have lunch sometime.

That evening, three of John's neighbors drop by. They've decided to meet once a week for Video Night; their goal is to systematically rent the American Film Institute's 100 greatest movies of all time—John found the list in last week's newspaper. This week it's the Marx Brothers in "Duck Soup." Next week it's "Ben Hur." Just before bedtime, John prays for the people he encountered today.

What can we learn from our fictional sower? At the start of the day, in his brief encounter with his neighbor at the end of the driveway, John did little more than inject the thought of God into a neighbor's mind. In the car pool, instead of jumping right in with *his* opinion about Jerry Springer, John was careful to ask Margaret for *hers*. Instead of disagreeing about Jerry Springer, they ended up agreeing about the need for guidance in marriage.

At work, John very naturally took an employee from Stephen Covey to C. S. Lewis, which could lead to any number of future opportunities for interaction. By visiting the man whose wife was ill, John showed that he was a human being—and in that setting, it was very natural to talk about God and prayer. John encouraged his fellow soccer coach to think about the game in a different light. With his Muslim co-worker, John took the role of the humble student; he decided to ask questions before he started giving answers. In the evening, John turned his television into a potential ministry tool—an idea that came to him as he read the morning paper with a sower's eyes.

Each person that John encountered is at a different stage of the sowing process. With each one he will continue to tend the soil until the person shows a willingness to talk openly and directly about the gospel. In some encounters John seemed to accomplish very little, as in the car pool situation. No matter; John knows that he will see Margaret and Joe Bob again every morning and evening, five days a week. The little victories that John experiences are *cumulative* victories.

By the way—my fictional account of a sower's day is not meant to create the impression that a sower is a nonstop ministry machine. John's fictional day was condensed for educational purposes; in reality, sowing is a very uneven activity. One day may be crowded with opportunities, and the next day nothing may happen at all. Some mornings, John may *sleep* in the car pool. The important lesson is that a sower is committed to nurture; to use daily opportunities, over an extended period of time, to encourage spiritual interest in everyone he meets.

Chapter 13 | SOWING IN THE MARKETPLACE

Have you heard this popular saying? "No one on his deathbed ever says, 'I wish I had spent more time at the office.'" This modern proverb is on its way to becoming a classic. In fact, only one thing keeps it from achieving timeless status as a Great Truth of Life.

It's not true.

In point of fact, many people on their deathbeds do regret not having spent more time at the office. Albert Einstein's last words to his son were: "If only I had more mathematics!" The French composer Ravel's final utterance was: "I still had so much music to write!" American engineer and inventor James Eads departed this world with: "I cannot die! I have not finished my work!" Charles Darwin voiced only one regret as he lay dying: "I am only sorry that I haven't the strength to go on with my research."[1]

Psychologists tell us that two of our most compelling needs are the need for love and the need to work. Sometimes in our hunger for fulfillment we confuse these two longings. A lonely middle-aged man immerses himself in his career, unconsciously hoping to find ac-

ceptance, appreciation, and admiration—hoping to be *loved*. But ultimately he feels unfulfilled in his work *and* unloved. His work seems
somehow unsatisfying, though his performance is outstanding.
There's still something missing, a kind of gut-level craving he can't
quite put his finger on, so he pours himself ever more deeply into his
profession. He has made the tragic mistake of seeking to meet his
need for love through work, and although work can be fulfilling and
meaningful, it simply cannot substitute for love.

In our fervor to counterbalance the career obsession of the eighties and nineties, we—especially men—have told ourselves that what
we *really* need is to go home. Consider a long line of movies from the
last twenty years: *Hook, Mrs. Doubtfire, Mr. Mom, Regarding Henry, City
Slickers, The River Wild,* and *One Fine Day.* Each has been the story of a
father's redemption—a redemption that takes place when an absentee
father is forced to reevaluate his life priorities, cast aside his workaholic
tendencies, and return in body and spirit to his family.

This message has been a badly needed counterbalance to our
society's overemphasis on work, but every counterbalance runs the
risk of creating a new unbalance. In this case, the new unbalance is
that we are now telling ourselves that to be truly fulfilled, *all we need* is
to go home. Happiness is not found in work, but in our marriages
and children and families. We will never regret leaving work undone;
we will *only* regret failing to love. Ambition—of all types—has become the bad guy. The extent to which you want to work is the extent to which You Don't Get It. Work is the *problem;* love is the *answer.*

Like most great errors, this message contains a partial truth. We
do need to remind ourselves of the importance of relationships, but
we must never forget that we possess a *dual* nature. We were designed
by God to love *and* to work. As important as relationships are, it is a
mistake to suggest that fulfillment is found through relationships
alone. Something deep within us, something placed there by God,
longs to fulfill itself through *doing*—but something has gone wrong
with the world of work.

Let's be honest—even for those of us who enjoy what we do,
there is sometimes more work than fulfillment. At its worst, work
can be boring, repetitive, and downright meaningless. So how does
work regain its rightful place in our lives? What can make our place
of employment a greater source of satisfaction? How can we begin

to transform forty hours of labor into forty hours of fulfillment? By learning to value our work as something given by God and learning to sow in the marketplace.

When "ministry in the marketplace" is mentioned, it often sends a shudder down the spine of the working Christian. That's because "ministry in the marketplace" translates as "harvesting in the marketplace," which conjures up images of finding clever ways to present the entire gospel to each co-worker. Although the workplace can be a difficult place to harvest, it's an ideal place to sow.

Introducing God into the World of Work

In chapters 8 through 11, I described what it means to sow in the life of an individual: to cultivate, plant, and nurture. To sow means to attempt to introduce God, in some way, into the life of every individual you regularly encounter. Many of those you regularly encounter you will find at the place where you invest fifty hours of every week—your place of work. All the skills of cultivating, planting, and nurturing can be applied on the job, as we saw in the example of the fictional John. But sowing in the marketplace requires a *prior* step. Before the sower can effectively and enthusiastically reach out to his business associates, he must first transform his attitude toward work itself. To put it another way, *before the sower can introduce his co-workers to God, he must introduce God into his work.*

For a gardener, sowing sometimes involves working nutrients deep into the soil so that a plant can put down an extensive root system. In the same way, the first step in sowing in the marketplace involves "working" God deep into the atmosphere of our workplace, until an environment is created where spiritual activity can naturally occur.

The Disconnection Between Work and Fulfillment

The Henry Ford Museum in Dearborn, Michigan, is a monument to the Industrial Revolution in America. Created by Henry Ford himself, it chronicles Ford's innovations that changed forever the nature of work in America. Ironically, next door to the Ford Museum is a different kind of monument—also created by Ford—called Greenfield Village. Named after Mrs. Ford's childhood community, Greenfield Village is an exact replica of a typical small town of the late nineteenth century. It was Ford's memorial to the simple, pre-industrial world that the automobile helped destroy forever. No one knew better than Henry Ford that the mass production assembly line had done far more than create a new product; it had changed the nature of life itself.

Ford's assembly line shortened the time needed to construct an automobile from 12.5 hours to just 1.5 hours, but this technical efficiency came at a high human price. As worker boredom increased, so did absenteeism. As production quotas continually increased, workers began to suffer stress-related ailments, and the incidence of alcoholism increased. In a short time, Ford found it difficult to keep enough workers on his assembly lines to meet his production schedule.

What went wrong? To put it simply, the Industrial Revolution completed a process that began at the Fall—the corruption of work. In the Garden man was separated from his Creator; on the assembly line man was separated from his work. Once, work was the deepest expression of who a person was; now, there was nothing of the person in his work—he became little more than an extension of the machine he operated.

Laborers often had little idea what their monotonous task contributed to the final product—in fact, from where most of them stood, they couldn't even see the end of the assembly line. Once, a worker might have felt esteemed as a respected craftsman in a field that required years of training and experience. Now, almost anyone could do almost any job. For the sake of productivity, something terrible had been sacrificed—*the meaning of work.*

Ford's solution to the lack of worker motivation was to more than double the average salary, from $2.34 for a nine-hour day to $5 for an eight-hour day. Ford's audacious offer more than solved his manpower problem. It made employment in his factory a sought-after prize. But even as he solved one problem, he created another. Ford's workers, through their boredom, stress, alcoholism, and absenteeism, were expressing their struggle with a single question: *What does my work mean?* Ford's answer: *Work means money.* And though the Model T has long since disappeared, Ford's simplistic answer to the meaning of work still torments many of us today.

The Original Meaning of Work

Work has *never* been chiefly about money. But if work is not about money, what in the world *is* it about? The first chapter of the book of Genesis gives us some clues. From the moment of their creation, men and women were assigned dual responsibilities: to increase in numbers (love) and to rule the earth (work). Chapter 2 relates that upon Adam's creation he was immediately placed in the Garden of Eden "to work it and take care of it" (Genesis 2:15 NIV). Contrary to common belief, work is not a curse or a result of the Fall, and a perfect world would not be a world of pure leisure. The desire to work—*and to find fulfillment in it*—is a part of our human design.

Imagine what it was like to work before the Fall. Adam and Eve had a clear sense that work was much more than something they *did*—it was an expression of what they *were*. They were aware that work was a responsibility assigned by their Creator, and that they were uniquely qualified to fill this role. As they labored, they knew that God was aware of their efforts, and they sensed His pleasure. At times His presence was so real that work seemed like a kind of partnership. Hard work produced clear and impressive results, and they had a deep inner sense of fulfillment. Thank God it's Monday!

But after the Fall a great change took place. God Himself withdrew from both relationships and work, and both love and labor were corrupted. As Adam and Eve lost their awareness of God's presence, they began to lose their sense of the purpose of their work. *Why* am I doing this? Why does this *matter?* They no longer felt God's pleasure exclusively, but now they also felt His anger and rejection. Work had little to do with fulfilling their design now; too often it had to do only with survival. Work had become much harder, and it seemed boring, repetitive, and futile. In short, work had lost much of its *meaning*.

The original, biblical meaning of work could be described this way: *Work means fulfilling your God-given design to make an impact on the world around you.* Adam was not assigned work as a punishment for his sin; on the contrary, he was *created* to work. His punishment was that he largely lost his ability to be *fulfilled* by his labor. From now on his work would take place in a hostile environment, involving painful toil and a nagging sense of futility. Just as sin has alienated us from one another, so sin has estranged us from our work, and it continues to do so.

The result is that we have divorced God from our work. We think of God the same way we think of the Bible; it's appropriate for Him to accompany us to church or a Bible study, but we leave Him on the coffee table when we head for the office on Monday morning. He just doesn't seem to belong there. After all, it's just *business,* and what does God care about business?

When a person becomes a Christian today, she tends to think of her conversion as a *personal* experience. The old things have passed away and new things have come—in her spirit, her emotions, her character, even in her relationships—but not in her job. She unconsciously thinks of the realm of business as a world apart, outside of the reach—or the interest—of God. Her Christianity is a self-contained world, confined to the spheres of church, marriage, friendships—confined to *spiritual* places.

Reclaiming God's Calling in the Workplace

Of course, conversion *is* an inward experience—but it's an outward experience, too, one that touches every area of being *and* doing. The early Puritans taught that when a person becomes a Christian, every place in the Christian's life becomes a spiritual place, including the place of work. The Puritans taught that Christ's lordship extends to every area of our lives, and the new Christian should stop thinking of his "work" and start thinking of his "vocation"—the specific way in which God has called him to have an impact on the world as a Christian. What a concept—"called" to a place of employment. We currently reserve the notion of calling to the "spiritual" professions. I've been *called* to the pastorate; I feel *called* to go to seminary; my *calling* is to the mission field. Imagine hearing someone say, "I've been called to work in middle management at IBM." Wait a minute! You can't say that. You can't be *called* to secular work; you just *choose* to work there. God calls only to the spiritual professions, but is strangely disinterested in all the others.

Not according to the Puritans. They taught that all professions are spiritual to the Christian, not because of the nature of the work *but because of the presence of God.* The ground around the burning bush was ordinary dirt; only the presence of God made it holy. When a

Christian—the temple of the Holy Spirit—walks into an office at IBM, IBM becomes a spiritual place.

The first step in sowing in the marketplace is a fundamental change in our attitude toward work, a change that can have remarkable results. We need to begin to see our places of employment as spiritual places, as places that God cares very much about, as places that God has *called* us to in order to represent Him. The most secular profession is in a sense something holy. God is as much present behind the counter at Taco Bell as He is in the pastor's study.

The impact of this change in mind-set is staggering. I no longer have a "job," or even that modern-day job replacement, a "career"—I have a *mission*. My mission is to seek to introduce God into every aspect of my occupation. My calling is to make an impact on my world by fleshing out my Christianity in *this* profession, at *this* department, with *these* co-workers. Instead of seeing leisure as the true source of fulfillment and Sunday as the place for God, my work can become a place for both. My work, no matter how inglorious, is no longer just about money—I have recovered the original meaning of work.

Think of it as "Taking God to Work with You." Several years ago, feminists began to encourage a program called "Take Your Daughter to Work with You." They urged businesspeople to create vision in their daughters by taking them along to their places of employment. What if, instead, we left for work each morning with *God* in our car pool? How would it change my day if I was conscious that my Creator shares my cubicle?

The obvious result of this change of perspective is a dramatic increase in enthusiasm for work. If my work is something I merely endure, looking to the weekend for challenge or fulfillment, then each workday I send only half of myself to work; my body gets on the bus, but my heart remains behind. But Paul tells me in Colossians that whatever I do, I should work at it with *all my heart* since—all appearances to the contrary—I am working for Christ and not men. It's sometimes hard to get excited about working for men, but working for God—just as Adam did in the garden—that's something else.

The first step in sowing in the marketplace is to "Take God to Work with You": to reintroduce God into your concept of work, to allow God to transform your job or career into a mission. That sim-

ple adjustment in attitude can make a profound impact on your enthusiasm for work. But a second step is required. You are not only
driven by the desire to express yourself through *doing,* but to express
yourself through doing something *unique to you.* The second step in
sowing in the marketplace is to learn to introduce God not simply
into work in general, but into *your specific job.*

Introducing God into Your Specific Job

The American journalist H. L. Mencken was asked at the age of
fifty-two, after achieving considerable success, why he was motivated
to go on working. His response: "I go on working for the same reason that a hen goes on laying eggs." He worked, Mencken said, because it was in his *nature* to work; just as for the hen, it was simply an
expression of who he was.

Of course the hen goes on laying eggs, not giving milk or
pulling a plow. In other words, it isn't simply the hen's nature to
work, but to do a specific *kind* of work. Mencken himself felt com-
pelled to express himself as a writer and a literary critic; when he
did, it seemed so natural to him that he could not imagine ever stopping. Perhaps this is the meaning of Proverbs 10:23: "Doing wicked-
ness is like sport to a fool, and so is wisdom to a man of
understanding." Work, when it truly fits us, may cease to be work at
all. "Find work that you love," the old adage says, "and you'll never
work a day in your life."

In their book *Your Work Matters to God,* Doug Sherman and
William Hendricks wrote:

> God has made you with a specific design. As one of His creatures,
> He has given you personal resources—a personality, talent, abilities,
> interests and so forth—which can be used vocationally. . . .
>
> It is clear you are not simply a random collection of molecules
> thrown together by chance. God has crafted you in a very unique and
> personal way. In terms of your vocation, this means that you are fit to
> do certain tasks.
>
> It therefore follows that the "right" job for you is one in which
> there is a good match between the way God has designed you and a
> job requiring someone with your abilities.[2]

Considering God's Calling in Your Vocation

When Adam was created, he was given a very general work assignment: to "subdue" the earth and to "rule over" it. His own children began to fulfill that generic responsibility in unique and individual ways. Cain followed in his father's footsteps as a farmer, but his brother Abel became a "keeper of flocks." Abel sought not only to fulfill God's general command, but also to fulfill his own design as a unique individual, very different from his father and brother. Note, by the way, that these were not "spiritual" professions—but callings necessary to sustaining life that were important in their own right.

This has been the challenge for Christians from the beginning—to understand how Christ relates to us as unique individuals and to our unique spheres of employment. In Luke 3, John the Baptist was preaching a message of repentance—a change of *doing*—to multitudes along the Jordan River, preparing the way for the Messiah who would follow. After the message, John's listeners lined up to ask questions about how John's admonitions should be applied *to their specific situations*. "What shall we do?" the tax collectors asked, and John gave them an application point specific to tax collectors. Soldiers came next: "And what about us?" they asked, implying that the advice given to the tax collectors did them little good. "What shall *we* do?" John then gave the soldiers advice on how God can be introduced into the unique world of the military.

Jesus' early hearers had the same response to His teachings. "What shall we do?" they commonly asked. They listened to Jesus' words not as churchgoers or spiritual leaders, but as simple working people. Jesus spoke to shepherds and farmers and fishermen and lawyers, and His words were applied to their spheres of work. "Half of my possessions I will give to the poor," the repentant tax collector Zaccheus concluded, "and if I have defrauded anyone of anything, I will give back four times as much" (Luke 19:8). Salvation had come to his house—and also to his specific work.

I recommend that we begin to think deeply—many of us for the first time—about what it means to be a Christian *in our specific job*. The challenge of introducing God into a specific job is easiest for those of us who work in professional ministry, not because our work is more spiritual, but because the New Testament gives us such a big head start. The Scriptures do the work for us; they give direct instructions about evangelism, discipleship, Bible study, fellowship, church discipline, and a dozen other topics that make up our daily work. Thanks to the Bible, we know what a Christian pastor or elder looks like—but after this point we enter a vast, uncharted territory. What in the world does a Christian *auto mechanic* look like?

The Bible doesn't answer that question. Jesus illustrated many of His teachings with examples from farming, which were familiar to His first-century listeners. But most of us have never been on a farm—we live in the Information Age. The question "What does it mean to be a Christian systems analyst?" is one that we will have to answer for ourselves.

To introduce God into our specific jobs, we need to think deeply about questions like these:

- What does it mean to both be a Christian *and* hold this job?
- How would I do my job differently if I were not a Christian?
- What biblical principles most apply to my daily responsibilities?
- How should my faith affect the way I relate to my co-workers, superiors, or employees?
- Do I know any experienced or successful Christians in this line of work? Is there a way I can benefit from their experience?
- Has anything been written by a Christian in this or a similar field?
- Can I meet with other Christians in my field to continue to explore these questions?

Meeting with Others in Your Vocation

In our churches, study and discussion groups form around traditional roles and interests. Marriage groups discuss how to be a better husband or wife, parenting groups study scriptural child-rearing principles, and recovery groups apply biblical wisdom to modern addictions and dependencies. Yet when was the last time you saw an accountants group or a managers workshop *in your church?* The concept sounds almost humorous, because we see these topics as belonging outside the scope of the church. But why is an accountants group any more ludicrous than a parenting group, when you consider that you spend just as many hours each week as an accountant as you do in active parenting? The topic in both groups is really the same—the application of Christianity to specific life settings.

The stark reality of life is that for most of us, forty to sixty hours of every week is spent at work. What a tragedy it is if we have to simply *endure* the best hours of our day and the best years of our lives, hoping to somehow wring fulfillment from the scraps left over at the end. Many of us, cut off from the fulfillment of work as God intended it, are willing to accept money as a substitute because money can allow us to seek fulfillment in some other arena of life—if there's any time left after work. It's a trade-off that's made by millions today. People count the hours until the weekend, the days until vacation, and the years until retirement.

It doesn't have to be this way, if only we will choose to reintroduce God into a world that was originally His. Once our attitude toward our work begins to change, we'll find it easy and natural to cultivate, plant, and nourish in our place of work. And once we begin to understand how our faith informs our *specific* form of work, we'll become the enthusiastic sowers we should be.

Our faith will first transform our own business ethics and practices. In 1997, American retailers reported that they lost more than nine billion dollars to shoplifting; in the same period, retailers estimate that they lost more than *ten* billion dollars to theft *by their own employees*. Such things can happen on the job—but they happen a lot less at your place of *mission*.

Your new perspective on work may also begin to influence your specific business decisions and even corporate policies. Chick-Fil-A is a corporation with a large number of dedicated Christians in positions of leadership. The "employment opportunity" posters at their local restaurants include the words, "Attention Moms! When your children have school off, you are not required to work!" I know of no way that policy can increase revenues—or reduce scheduling headaches—for Chick-Fil-A. It's simply an example of a Christian worldview being expressed through a family-friendly corporate policy.

The most important transformation will be a change in attitude toward your co-workers. The world of *work* is a competitive, dog-eat-dog world of self-promotion and one-upmanship. The world of *mission* is a world of service, compassion, and cooperation.

That doesn't mean that a sower can't seek to advance himself or maintain a competitive attitude; it means that the sower recognizes that more is going on around him than work—*much* more.

Work is where life is played out. Our co-workers come to the office each day with struggling marriages, rebelling children, financial worries, health scares, and a thousand other cares and concerns that can't be left in the driveway when they leave for work each morning. Most of these people we will *only* see at the office. When most people return home at night, they are immersed in their family's activities and protective of their few hours off. That means that the marketplace is a rare opportunity to cross paths with a wide variety of people that we will have access to in no other place.

The nature of the workplace makes it a difficult place to harvest. Each workday is busy, and our interactions with others are often reduced to a phone call, an e-mail, a brief planning meeting, or a quick lunch. That's a tough place to harvest—but it's a great place to sow. As the sower continues to "Take God to Work" each morning he will develop the habit of one-minute missions—seizing those fleeting opportunities to cultivate, plant, and nurture on the job.

Chapter 14 | SOWING TO THE CULTURE

Have you ever wanted to know and do God's will?" Those are the first words of Henry Blackaby's popular book *Experiencing God*. According to Blackaby, the key to discovering God's will is not to focus on your own life, but on the work that God seems to be doing in the world around you. "[God] does not ask us to dream our dreams for Him and then ask Him to bless our plans," he cautioned. "He is already at work when He comes to us. His desire is to get us from where we are to where He is working. When God reveals to you where He is working, that becomes His invitation to join Him."[1]

I believe this is an excellent principle—but also a very dangerous one. Before this principle can be applied, a very important question must be answered—a question so important that, if answered incorrectly, will lead to a tragic misapplication of the principle itself.

How do you know where God is working?

There's an old joke about a man walking down a street late one night, when he came across another man. The second man was down on his hands and knees under a streetlight, busily searching for something. Their conversation went something like this:

"What are you looking for?"

"My car keys."

"Where did you lose them?"

"Down there, in that dark alley."

"Then why in the world are you looking for them here?"

"Because the light's better here."

The moral of the story: We often look for answers where we *want* to find them, not where they really *are*.

Where does the average evangelical believe God is really *working?* Answer: wherever things are *happening*. Wherever there is *action*. Wherever there is *harvest*. To most evangelicals, who are very action-oriented people, the true sign of God's presence is *results*. Where God is, things happen, and when there is no action, God is obviously at work somewhere else. Blackaby himself admitted that "We are a 'doing' people. We always want to be doing something. The idea of doing God's will sounds fairly exciting."[2] Of course! The harvest is a lot more exciting than the hard, patient background work that produces it. But is God only at work in the harvest?

Was God at work in the life of John the Baptist, or did the real work only begin when Jesus arrived on the scene? Was God more at work in the life of Isaiah, who saw *results,* than in the life of Jeremiah, who saw none? Are there "down times" in history, times in which God is not really active? Was the period between the Testaments a kind of four-hundred-year half-time for God, after which He burst back onto the playing field in the Gospels?

The problem we face today is that the average, action-oriented evangelical, seeking to know and do the will of God, often goes through a thought process like this: *To do the will of God, I must find out where God is working and join Him there. Nothing seems to be happening here, but there's plenty of action over there. Obviously, God is at work over there, so that's where I must go to join Him.*

The result is that we become like migrant workers, constantly moving on in search of a bigger and better harvest. In the Dust Bowl era, migrant workers piled into their crumbling jalopies and headed for California. In our day of high-tech travel and global communication, we can locate distant harvests anywhere on the planet and quickly redirect our energy and resources toward these spiritual "hot spots"—the places where God is *really* at work.

It's important that the reader not misunderstand. There *are* spiritual hot spots, temporary windows of opportunity where a people group shows itself to be unusually open to the gospel. In those situations, it's perfectly appropriate for ministries to redirect their energies to attempt to reap the harvest while the window remains open. My concern is that we've come to believe that God is *more* at work in these places—*more at work in harvesting than in sowing.*

America is not the same place of harvest that it was forty years ago. Who wants to stay behind to do useless work in a place that God Himself has abandoned? Those are strong words, but I don't use those words carelessly. More and more churches and ministries speak as though America has had its chance, and now God is turning His attention and blessing to other nations. Perhaps America is no longer the preeminent place of harvest on our planet, but that gives us no right to abandon our culture entirely in pursuit of easier harvests. After doing the comparatively easy work of the harvest, will we now refuse to sow?

Consider again a few of the major cultural trends that I've described earlier in this book:

- Our culture is rapidly changing. The increasing emphasis on tolerance and pluralism is creating a growing hostility toward conservative Christians.

- Christians believe that America, once a Christian nation, is being taken away from us. We feel attacked, and as a result we tend to adopt a culture war mind-set.

- We prefer to take the role of the prophet, preferring justice to love. We emphasize courage and boldness more than wisdom and tact.

- The Christian attitude toward our culture tends to be separatist. We seek to be innocent as doves, but often fail to be shrewd as serpents.

- Convinced that these are the end times, we adopt a burn-over mentality. We see no reason to plan ahead in a world that has no future.

• Due to the successful harvest of recent decades, we now see harvesting as the only legitimate form of ministry. We devalue sowing as slow, unspiritual, or even cowardly.

The effect of these trends can be summarized in four simple points:

• Christians are retreating from the culture, taking an adversarial attitude.
• The non-Christian culture is becoming more hostile in return.
• The culture, from a Christian perspective, is eroding rapidly.
• If Christians don't begin to sow, we've seen our last harvest.

What Christians most need to understand is that, in our confidence that these are the last days, *we are betting the farm*—and to put it bluntly, it's a gamble we can't afford. Martin Luther was once asked what he would do if he knew for certain that the world would end tomorrow. He replied, "I would plant a tree today." Luther implied that a Christian must *always* have one foot in the future. We should live in the constant hope of Christ's imminent return, but plan and work as though He won't come back for a long, long time. That means that Christians today must resist their myopic tendencies and look to the future. We must begin the long, long process of sowing to our culture.

Reinvesting in Our Culture

As I see it, Christians face the same concerns as those who are involved in the environmental movement. The environmentalist shouts to the logger and the developer, "You ignore the environment to your own doom, because *you* are a part of the environment!" Regardless of the anger or hostility we might feel toward our culture, we must remember that *we are a part of that culture*. We cannot simply withdraw, because our fates are intertwined. The condition of the culture directly affects our ability to live, work, and worship as Christians. If our society at large becomes hostile to Christianity, we will suffer, as history readily testifies.

The environmentalist offers a second warning: "We don't inherit the world from our parents; we borrow it from our kids." We have a responsibility to the *next* generation. *We* have resources aplenty to live comfortably in *this* generation, but if we refuse to replenish the environment, we pass on a ravaged and barren landscape to our children. It must be a slow, expensive, and bothersome task for foresters to replant felled forests with tiny seedlings. Why bother? The foresters will never live to see those trees mature—but their sons and daughters will. In the same way, in every ministry strategy and evangelistic campaign we mount we should ask ourselves, "What effect might this have on the *next* generation of Christians?"

But *where* is the Christian to reinvest in the culture? Every environmentalist knows that you can't give back to the environment on a one-to-one basis; you can't plant one tree for every tree felled. The environmentalist has to think wisely about how to invest in the areas that will bring the maximum return. What are those areas for the Christian?

Thirty years ago, Francis Schaeffer wrote a book entitled *The God Who Is There,* in which he described a major philosophical shift that took place in our country in this century. The shift itself is not important here; what *is* important is the way in which Schaeffer believed this new way of thinking worked its way into everyday thought. He believed that the philosophical shift entered our culture through a series of disciplines: It began in philosophy, then it spread to the arts, then went to the world of popular music, followed by the general culture, where it was finally picked up by theologians.[3] Schaeffer believed that each of these disciplines plays an influential role in spreading new ideas to our culture, directly affecting the atmosphere in which Christians live and work. These disciplines, then, are crucial places for Christians to begin to sow.

Expanding slightly on Schaeffer's list, let me suggest a series of areas where Christians must begin to reinvest in our culture:

- **The Media:** Film, television, electronic news, cyberpublishing, print publishing
- **The Arts:** Theater, the traditional arts, performance arts
- **Music:** Writing, performance, and production

- **The Humanities:** History, literature, cultural studies
- **Academics:** Research, teaching at all levels, curriculum development
- **Politics:** National, state, and local levels
- **Corporate Business:** Management, human resources, etc.

What does the sower invest in one of these areas? To put it simply: *his or her life.* It will require no less. In chapter 12, I said that to become a truly effective sower in the marketplace, the Christian must discover a sense of God's calling to his place of work—he must develop a sense of *mission.* Sowers must develop that same sense of mission toward a specific discipline or institution. We must be willing to invest the time—the *years*—necessary to become an insider, and to sow faithfully over the course of a lifetime. One thing is certain—none of the disciplines I've listed above will ever be significantly changed by an occasional visitor.

Cultivating the American Soil

But how does the Christian *specifically* begin to sow within one of these fields? The problem is, there is no one answer to that question—and in many of these fields few Christians have yet been there to pave the way. I believe that sowing to the American culture will be the great missionary strategy of the next century—I believe it *must* be. An entire movement of Christians must catch a vision for cultivating the American soil. They must be willing to invest their lives in a task that currently has no value in the eyes of their brethren—the long, slow, behind-the-scenes work of creating a national environment where the gospel can take root. Though I can't show a clear, paved path to that goal, I *can* describe seven essentials that will be necessary for the task to be completed.

1. We Must Revalue the Role of the Sower

The most difficult challenge that faces us is the first. Christians must first expand our view of ministry to include the task of sowing; after that, we must honor and esteem those who choose to fill that role. That won't be easy. Right now, harvesters are preoccupied with "beseeching the Lord to send out laborers into His harvest." Harvesting organizations, like the one I work for, are always recruiting fellow harvesters, and we are always acutely aware of the shortage of new laborers. Since there never seem to be enough workers to meet the needs of the *harvest,* it's hard to encourage talented and available Christians to spend their time *sowing*—but encourage them we must. Even if organizations like my own had an *unlimited* supply of harvesters, *there would still be a critical need for sowers.* The need to sow in our nation is not the result of some failure on the part of harvesters who didn't do their job quickly or aggressively enough; it is simply the result of the passing of time and changing cultural conditions.

Right now, our churches and ministries hope and pray that the Christians we train will enter the pastorate or mission field. We rejoice over those who do—those are our success stories. We pay little attention to those who don't—those are our "also-rans." This must change. From our first moment of contact with a young Christian, we must help him understand God's sovereign claim to his life. We must help him understand that he has been called to be a laborer, and that both sowing and harvesting are options—*valuable* options— open to him. If sowing is the option he chooses, we must equip him and encourage him with all the zeal that we would show the aspiring missionary.

2. We Must Talk Within Our Churches About How to Sow

The only ministry skills that are taught in our churches are the skills of the harvester. A church hosts an evangelism-training program; parishioners are taught to use a basic evangelistic tool like the Romans Road. Then they are sent out, duly admonished to put this training to use with their neighbors and friends. The problem is, they don't, at least according to statistics. I suspect that many of them leave the training program thinking, *My friends aren't ready for this, I don't know my neighbors well enough, and I could never get away with this at work.* Equipped only with the skills of the harvester, they continue on in guilty silence, telling themselves that one of these days they are going to walk right up to a neighbor and put that training to use. One of these days.

We must begin to train Christians how to cultivate, plant, and nurture, and that training must begin in our churches. We must talk about how to ask good questions and how to build agreements instead of arguments. We must talk about books, tapes, music, and movies that a sower can recommend to a non-Christian—and we must begin to stock these materials in our church libraries alongside *Left Behind*. In short, we must learn together how to be effective sowers, and as our skills grow we must share this knowledge with other churches.

3. We Must Train Our Youth in the Philosophy and Basic Skills of Sowing.

Sowing is a long-term process, and the sooner we learn the skills of the sower, the sooner the process can begin. We can greatly ease the process if we will begin to help our children understand the role of the sower from a very young age. Long before a child is ready to be a trained harvester, he can be a very effective sower; in fact, children seem to do it very well by instinct. Children have an unaffected openness and honesty about spiritual things that make conversation with others very natural. If we can only recognize and encourage those skills, we can begin now to equip a whole generation of outstanding sowers.

4. We Must Encourage Training and Education for Advanced Areas of Sowing.

The harvester's most successful trainee is a candidate for the ministry or an applicant to seminary. The sower's most successful trainee might be an applicant to USC Film School or a candidate for political office. The harvester's trainee may receive funding, ongoing guidance, and encouragement; the sower's trainee deserves no less. As we broaden our view of ministry to include sowing, we will need to broaden the base of services and financial assistance we provide to include sowers.

This suggestion raises some practical difficulties. How could churches afford to do this? I'm not suggesting, of course, that churches begin to give scholarships to every student who wants to go to college or graduate school just because the student could one day be in a position to sow. That would be tantamount to funding everyone, since virtually everyone can be a sower, from the president of a large corporation to the office secretary who interacts with only two or three co-workers a day. We can't fund everyone—but as we encourage the work of sowers within our churches, it will become clear that certain individuals have special talents and abilities, and some may express an interest in a ministry of sowing at a very high level or in a very strategic field. These strategic people—the potential Esthers and Wilberforces of the future—are the ones we should help.

Imagine a talented young Christian whose life dream is to be a major network anchorperson. In our current mind-set we would encourage him to begin the "outward spiral" described in chapter 6. Would he like to study broadcasting at a Bible college? Would he like to work for "The 700 Club" "someday? If the answer is no to both questions, we're out of options and he's on his own. It rarely occurs to us that any assistance we could give a devoted Christian in becoming a major news anchor could be an incredibly good investment of our time and resources. That assistance will have to take new and nontraditional forms, like encouraging internships at secular corporations and providing financial assistance for education at secular colleges.

To be fair, the sower has one distinct advantage over the harvester: Unlike the career missionary, the sower's eventual mission field will in all likelihood pay a salary that can support him financially. At that time, the sower should of course be financially on his own. But until the sower reaches that point, he may need financial assistance to receive the education or training to reach his intended place of service. His need is as legitimate as that of the missionary—if we consider sowing an equally legitimate form of ministry.

5. We Must Create Support Structures for Our Sowers

Nothing is harder than the task you have to do *alone*—and no word describes the sower's current status better. "Encourage one another," Paul instructed us, and support structures must be created to keep sowers equipped and motivated for their work. Sowers need three forms of support: equipping, encouraging, and esteem. Equipping means training sessions and discussion groups, sponsored and encouraged by the church, where sowers can continue to build their skills. Encouragement can be provided through the fellowship of other sowers: meetings, prayer sessions, and even parties where fellow sowers in a common field can meet to challenge and encourage one another. Esteem is something that must be provided by the church leadership. Visiting missionaries give sermons in our churches; do visiting sowers? Young Christians leaving for seminary or mission projects are honored or commissioned by the church leadership; could the same be done for a young sower leaving for a summer internship at DuPont? Sowers will need to know, by word and by deed, that their ministry is recognized *and valued* by those in authority.

6. We Must Prepare for the Long Haul

The most difficult change in attitude for Christians will be the shift from a short-term to a long-term view of ministry—in some cases, a *very* long-term view. I'm amazed to hear how ministries sometimes talk about their plans to reach some specific group or discipline within our culture: We are going to *take back* the university, we are going to *revolutionize* the film industry. Who are we kidding? We still speak in the revolutionary jargon of the sixties, as if deeply entrenched institutions can be seized and overthrown overnight. It didn't work in the sixties, and it won't work that way today. When attempting to influence any institution or discipline, Christians first need to do a reality check. How long did it take this discipline to get the way it is today? How deeply does it hold its current convictions and values? What would it actually require to bring about change in this institution as a whole?

Consider a single discipline like philosophy. The current state of philosophical thought in America has some of its roots in the Enlightenment. Thousands of minds have contributed to the development of philosophy in this century alone. No simple program or appeal is going to reverse that process overnight. That's why the sower who wants to reinvest in the culture must be willing to dedicate his *life* to the task. Philosophical trends are created by dedicated scholars with graduate degrees who have given their lives to the study of philosophy. Those who wish to bring about change in their world will have to do the same.

It's interesting to note that many of the sixties radicals who once advocated revolution and the overthrow of the system are now *part* of the system. That isn't to say that they gave up all of their radical ideals; some of them simply chose to go about their goals in a different way. They chose to sow, and to do so they had to agree to invest their lives in a slow, long-term process of working from within the system. Perhaps we can learn something from them.

7. We Must Be Willing to Accept Unmeasurable Results

The reality of life is that churches and parachurch organizations depend on fund-raising for their survival. Because ministry is not a profit-generating venture, ministries must constantly seek financial assistance to do what they do. When it comes to a competition for available funding, the harvester has a decided advantage over the sower. Nothing appeals to a potential donor like *results*. It's very appealing to be able to report, "At our most recent evangelistic presentation, 120 people attended and 30 prayed to receive Christ." Some evangelistic organizations actually have it figured out on a per capita basis: For every hundred dollars you invest, this many people will come to Christ. It's less impressive for the sower to report, "I've been talking with a lot of people, and each one is coming along quite nicely, thank you." Because ministries know that they are accountable for the use of their finances, they have a strong desire to quantify the results of their work: *This* is what we produced; *these* are our results.

But anyone who has worked for an evangelistic organization knows how uncertain those results are. How many *true* non-Christians attended our presentation? How many "decisions for Christ" were made by Christians who were simply indicating a recommitment? How many decisions were genuine? How many of these people will we ever see again?

A basic axiom of ministry is: *If you work in ministry, you must be willing to accept the fact that you will never know exactly what you are producing.* Jesus reminded us that tares are almost impossible to distinguish from wheat, and it will take God to sort it all out in the end. That shouldn't discourage us from harvesting—and it shouldn't discourage us from sowing, either. *All* forms of ministry are ultimately *unmeasurable,* but that doesn't render them *unvaluable.* To embrace the ministry of sowing, we will have to recognize the value of something that refuses to be quantified or measured.

Preparing for Future Harvests

As I said in chapter 1, this book is a call to a new generation of sowers to help reclaim our eroding soil and begin to prepare the harvest of the future. Sowing is not some trendy new approach to evangelism; it is an ancient, *biblical* approach to ministry that was recognized and valued by Jesus Himself. The purpose of this book is not to *invent* sowing, but to remind Christians that it has *always* existed. In our hurry to harvest before the end of the age, we have simply forgotten about it.

Sowing is not an option. It is an essential task made even more necessary by the changing condition of the American fields. To be sure, we can refuse to sow; but just like the farmer in my opening parable, we will do so to our peril. Christians have experienced the best of times in America. Many refuse to believe that we could also experience the worst of times, right here at home.

I'm calling for a movement of sowers to commit their lives to the rebuilding of the American culture. Many Christians today, weary of our culture's foolish excesses, are proclaiming that America has had its chance. *We have no right to that judgment.* We are expected to grant forgiveness to individuals not seven times, but seventy times seven. Can we offer less to our nation as a whole?

I'm calling for Christians to rise to a whole new level of energy, persistence, and wisdom: energy to pursue a culture that's rapidly retreating from us; persistence to work diligently while waiting for long-term results; and wisdom to know how to speak boldly, yet with gentleness and reverence.

I'm calling for the pursuit of a distant harvest, a long-term commitment to reverse the trends that are stifling the harvest today. I'm calling for a strategic alliance between sowers and harvesters that will give Americans the greatest possible opportunity to hear and respond to the gospel. I'm calling for Christians to harvest *and* sow, as Jesus originally intended, so that one day the sower and the harvester will be glad together.

Chapter 15 | GOOD QUESTIONS ANSWERED

Q: *You speak of an overemphasis on courage today. Isn't there a real need for courageous Christians in this day and age?*

A: We could *all* use more courage. My concern is what happens when courage begins to be valued for its *own* sake. When Christians feel that they are being threatened, that they are being attacked and must fight to defend themselves, then courage takes on greater importance. But when courage takes on *supreme* importance, when it becomes our *highest* value, then we begin to do things for the sake of courage alone—or the *appearance* of courage. All of our ministry efforts are evaluated in terms of their courage quotient: Is this the *courageous* thing to do? Will this develop more *courage* in our people? Like the example of the youth group doing street preaching, we sometimes communicate in an unnecessarily rude or insensitive style simply because it appears more bold and daring.

Q: *Are you suggesting that harvesters are unloving and concerned only with justice?*

A: A good harvester should be just as motivated by love as the sower is. My point is that justice—a focus on God's requirements and what is expected of the harvester—often shapes the *form* of the harvester's message. The harvester often determines his message by simply asking, "What does God want said?" This is a vital concern, but I'm suggesting that this question be balanced by love—by also asking the question, "What can this person hear?" God Himself would want His message given in such a way; we represent His love as well as His justice. This balance will keep our communication from appearing self-centered, pushy, or insensitive. Jesus demonstrated a concern for both love *and* justice, and so must we.

Q: *You seem to favor persuasion over proclamation. Isn't there a time for a Christian to just take a stand?*

A: There certainly is. My concern is that too many Christians believe it's *always* that time. In Acts 13, Paul arrived in Pisidian Antioch on a Sabbath day. He went into the synagogue, as was his custom, to reason with them from the Scriptures. When he was finished, "the people kept begging that these things might be spoken to them the next Sabbath." The following week, Paul returned to find a huge crowd awaiting him. "But when the Jews saw the crowds, they were filled with jealousy and began contradicting the things spoken by Paul, and were blaspheming." At that point Paul "took a stand." He "spoke out boldly" and told them quite bluntly that he was turning to the Gentiles instead (Acts 13:42, 45–46). He didn't assume the disinterest of his hearers and speak in a confrontative manner right up front. Paul's approach was to reason and persuade as long as it was possible, and *then* to take a stand. That's a good rule of thumb for us today.

Q: *The problem with the concept of sowing is that it takes so much time. Doesn't this approach to ministry slow things down?*

A: Sowing may appear to be slow because it seems to accomplish only small changes at a time in the life of each individual. But at the same time, the sower seeks to accomplish *something* in the life of *every individual he meets.* Think of it this way: a sower and a harvester go out to minister together. The harvester asks himself, *Who looks ready to hear the gospel?* Nine people look indifferent or hostile; the tenth finally looks interested, so the harvester begins a conversation with him—which may be welcome or may not. In the meantime, the sower has had *some* conversation with *all nine others*—conversations which the sower will attempt to build on when he returns on a regular basis. Which ministry is proceeding faster?

Q: *Are you saying that if I meet a person who is in favor of abortion, I should always let that issue pass? Isn't that an issue that's important to God, too?*

A: That issue is most definitely important to God—in the right time and place. When a Christian wants to try to persuade an unbeliever, I suggest that the Christian first ask himself a simple question: "What do I want from this person?" The answer for many Christians is, "Everything." We want him to change his mind about Jesus, politics, and profanity. We want to bring a *completely transformed person* into the kingdom—but that's simply too much to ask. Our goal should be to introduce the person to Christ and to allow the Holy Spirit to complete the total transformation over time. If our goal is for a person to receive Christ, then we need to focus on that issue. The question here is not whether the subject of abortion is important, but whether it is important *when we are discussing the gospel.* When considering whether or not to include *any* topic along with the gospel, I recommend that the Christian ask himself two questions: "Is this issue *central* to the gospel itself?" and "Will this issue help me get *to* the gospel, or will it become a distraction *from* it?" When is the time to talk about abortion? *When our goal is to persuade the unbeliever about abortion.* We should always keep in mind the goal of our discussion and resist the constant temptation to be sidetracked from our goal.

Q: *Sowing seems to require so much knowledge of our neighbors and time spent with them. Given the busyness of modern life, isn't sowing impractical?*

A: Given the busyness of modern life, *all* forms of ministry seem impractical at times. Which form of ministry best fits the lifestyle and relationships of the average Christian today? A harvester's lifestyle requires that the Christian seek to initiate complete presentations of the gospel with neighbors and co-workers who are often near-strangers to him. It's a bit awkward to initiate a twenty-minute gospel presentation with someone you've barely spoken to before. As a result, harvesting sometimes seems to be a bold and efficient form of ministry that no one will do. The sower's lifestyle, on the other hand, requires that the Christian try to say *something* with everyone he regularly meets. That's much less awkward, and it becomes less awkward over time. Long-term, the sower may have to invest much more time in each person—but there is also a much greater chance that he will actually do so.

Q: *Why do we have to pay all this attention to sowing and preparing people? Can't God produce a harvest anytime He wants?*
A: C. S. Lewis was once asked why anyone should bother to pray to God. Why does God need us to tell Him anything when He already knows everything? Lewis responded that God doesn't need farmers to make food, either. In other words: It's not an issue of what God *can* do, but how He *chooses* to work on a regular basis. It's quite true that at any time that God pleases He can produce a harvest, regardless of our role in the process. God *can* do it without us—but most of the time He chooses not to. "Always be prepared to give an answer to everyone who asks you to give the reason for the hope that you have," Peter instructed us—then he added the reminder, "but do this with gentleness and respect . . ." (1 Peter 3:15b NIV). Why do gentleness and respect matter? Because on a regular basis, God seeks to produce a harvest *through* our involvement, and the style of that involvement seems to make a difference.

Q: *You say you work with Campus Crusade, a harvesting organization if ever there was one. Are you saying that organizations like yours should stop harvesting and start sowing?*
A: Not at all. It's perfectly appropriate for an organization to specialize and to declare itself primarily a harvesting organization.

I'm not arguing that harvesting is no longer valuable, but that *another* form of ministry is valuable, too. Campus Crusade, and other organizations like it, have done a tremendous service to the cause of Christ through aggressive harvesting. But two things are important for an organization like mine to remember. First, in our enthusiasm for harvesting, we must not devalue the role of the sower—this is a very real temptation for us. Second, we must remember that each specific field will tell us what kind of labor is now required. We can insist on harvesting, but we cannot insist on harvesting *this* field *right now,* if this field is not ripe for harvest. In those areas, Campus Crusade can step aside and encourage the work of sowers, or it can practice some sowing skills itself—which it often does.

Q: *Couldn't your concept of sowing be used by some Christians as a rationale for not confronting nonbelievers boldly? Couldn't sowing simply become an excuse for cowardice?*

A: Indeed it could, just as boldness and courage can become excuses for laziness and insensitivity. The harvester who stands on the street corner and shouts the gospel in an angry tone may think he is demonstrating courage, but his "courage" may simply be an excuse for a lack of compassion. The Scriptures teach that Christians have been granted great freedom in Christ; Peter warns us not to let that freedom become a "covering for evil" (1 Peter 2:16). Apparently, many good things can serve as coverings for baser motives. Both sowing *and* harvesting can be abused, depending on the heart of the individual Christian. True, biblical sowing requires a great deal of boldness and courage. Remember, the sower attempts to reach out in some way to everyone he sees on a regular basis. That could include a wide variety of individuals from incredibly diverse backgrounds. In some ways, a good sower requires more courage than a harvester.

Q: *Isn't there a sense in which Christians are "called out" from the world? Aren't we supposed to separate ourselves in some ways?*

A: We *are* to separate ourselves in some ways—in matters of the heart and mind, and in our morality and ethics. But many Christians are convinced that the only way to accomplish this is to withdraw from the world *entirely*. R. C. Sproul once wrote, "It was [Martin] Luther who declared that a new Christian must withdraw from the world FOR A SEASON, but upon reaching spiritual maturity must embrace the world as the theater of redemptive activity. His message was, 'Away with the cowards who flee from the real world and cloak their cowardice with piety.'"[1] Jesus never ceased to love God with all of His heart and mind, and He never compromised His standards—yet He reached out to sinners, tax gatherers, and prostitutes. We must be careful not to separate ourselves more than our Master did. Our goal should be to be like Him—*in* the world, but not *of* the world.

Q: *Isn't it likely that sowers and harvesters will end up in competition with one another? Doesn't this distinction in ministry methods set us up for division?*

A: Not if sowers and harvesters understand the complementary nature of their roles. The greatest potential for competition is over resources—specifically over available laborers. As I said before, harvesters are always short on manpower. What harvester will want to give up a talented and willing laborer to sowing? This apparent competition for resources is resolved when we realize that the *vast* majority of Christians will *never* take part in a harvesting style of ministry. On the other hand, sowing has the potential to involve huge numbers of Christians who never considered involvement in ministry before. Sowers don't need to compete for the harvester's resources—they can generate their own.

Q: *Jesus told us to beseech the Lord to send out laborers into His harvest. If sowing is so important, why didn't he mention praying for more sowers?*

A: For the same reason that a farmer, during harvest season, says very little about plowing or weeding. *It's not the time.* Jesus' ministry marked the beginning of an unprecedented harvest season, and it was time to concentrate on the harvest. But if Jesus was *only* concerned about the harvest, why did He call the disciples aside in John 4 to remind them of the debt they owed the sowers who had come before them? Why did He bother to point out that the disciples were entering into someone else's labor and that someone else had already done the hard work? John, in the last verse of his gospel, tells us that "There are also many other things which Jesus did, which if they were written in detail, I suppose that even the world itself would not contain the books that would be written." Of all that John *could* have recorded, why did he choose to tell us about the sower?

Q: *You speak of sowers and harvesters as if they're always two different kinds of people. Can't one person sow and harvest?*

A: Absolutely. *All* Christians should sow and harvest. I only picture the sower and the harvester as different people to emphasize the differences between the roles. Every sower should learn the basic skills of harvesting—how to give a clear, concise presentation of the gospel and how to invite a person to receive Christ. If he lacks this skill, he's doomed to forever sow but never harvest. The sower also needs the *boldness* of a harvester—or he'll be afraid to push his interactions with others to ever-deeper levels. In the same way, every harvester should learn some basic sowing skills—or in today's culture he'll find he has a lot of extra time on his hands. Every Christian should see himself as a *laborer,* and should be ready and willing to do *whatever* task the fields require.

Q: *You picture the sixties as a time of great harvest, and today as a time to sow. But don't harvesters still see results today?*

A: I'm not claiming that the harvest that began in the sixties is completely over. I'm simply observing what many others have noted, that the fields of our country are changing. There are still notable pockets of harvest in the United States—but there is also no denying that the general attitude of our culture toward Christianity is shifting fast. My concern is that our exclusive focus on harvesting will force us into ever-smaller pockets of activity—pockets that are far removed from the mainstream of our culture. Our society is being changed most by those who are farthest from the gospel—and those groups are often the most resistant to harvesting forms of ministry. To ignore these people is to abandon the culture entirely. We must embrace any ministry method that will allow us to interact with those who most oppose us—in other words, we have to sow.

NOTES

Chapter Two: Earthquake

1. Eric Miller, ed., *Future Vision: The 189 Most Important Trends of the 1990's* (Naperville, Ill.: Sourcebooks, 1991), 11.

2. George Barna, *Evangelism That Works* (Ventura, Calif.: Regal, 1995), 45.

3. Census Bureau, 9 April 1998.

4. Miller, *Future Vision*, 19.

5. William Crockett and James Sigountos, eds., *Through No Fault of Their Own? The Fate of Those Who Have Never Heard* (Grand Rapids: Baker, 1991), 258.

6. John Gray, "The Virtues of Toleration," *National Review,* 5 October 1992: 28.

7. Stephen Carter, *The Culture of Disbelief: How American Law and Politics Trivialize Religious Devotion* (New York: Anchor Books, 1993), 23.

Chapter Three: Calling Down Fire

1. Em Griffin, *The Mind Changers: The Art of Christian Persuasion* (Wheaton, Ill.: Tyndale, 1976), 31.

2. William Booth, "The Myth of the Melting Pot: America's Racial and Ethnic Divides," *The Washington Post,* 22 February 1998: A01.

3. Deborah Tannen, *The Argument Culture: Moving from Debate to Dialogue* (New York: Random House, 1998), 3–4.

4. John Woodbridge, "Culture War Casualties: How Warfare Rhetoric Is Hurting the Work of the Church," *Christianity Today,* 6 March 1995: 22–23.

5. C. S. Lewis, *The Screwtape Letters* (New York: Macmillan, 1982), 137–38.

6. C. S. Lewis, "Learning in War-Time," *The Weight of Glory and Other Addresses* (New York: Macmillan, 1980), cited in *The Essential C. S. Lewis* (New York: Macmillan, 1988), 371–77.

Chapter Four: The Sower's Art

1. This story is adapted from a story that appeared in the Orange County Edition of the *Los Angeles Times* some ten years ago.

2. Eugene Peterson, "Masters of Imagination," *Subversive Spirituality* (Grand Rapids: Eerdmans, 1997), 134.

3. Philip Yancey, *Open Windows* (Nashville: Nelson, 1985), 107.

4. Peterson, "Novelists, Pastors, and Poets," *Subversive Spirituality,* 180.

Chapter Five: Indirect Communication

1. Bevin Alexander, *How Great Generals Win* (New York: Norton, 1993), back cover.

2. Eugene Peterson, "On Pentecostals, Poets, and Professors," *Subversive Spirituality* (Grand Rapids: Eerdmans, 1997), 253.

3. Cited in Robert Byrne, ed., *1,911 Best Things Anybody Ever Said* (New York: Fawcett Columbine, 1988), 368.

4. C. S. Lewis, "Christian Apologetics," *God in the Dock: Essays on Theology and Ethics* (Grand Rapids: Eerdmans, 1970), 93.

5. Ibid.

6. Peterson, "Subversive Spirituality," *Subversive Spirituality,* 241.

7. Ben Nyberg, *The Best Writing on Writing* (Cincinnati: Story Press, 1994), 129–30.

8. Philip Yancey, *Open Windows* (Nashville: Nelson, 1985), 111.

9. Tony Campolo, "Getting Out of the World Alive," *Discipleship Journal* (Issue 86).

Chapter Six: Outside-In

1. Ernest Volkman, "H. A. R. Philby: The Mole's Mole," *Spies: The Secret Agents Who Changed the Course of History* (New York: John Wiley & Sons, 1994), 8.

Chapter Seven: Innocents Abroad

1. Exodus 34:7 NIV.

2. Proverbs 21:12 NIV.

3. Adapted from Luke 10:30–35.

4. William Bennett, *The Book of Virtues* (New York: Simon & Schuster, 1993), 141.

5. *The Expositor's Bible Commentary*, vol. 8, s.v. "Matthew 10:5b–16."

6. Reggie White, "Reggie's Offense," interview by Peggy Wehmeyer, *20/20 Monday* (ABC Transcript #1804: 27 April 1998), 11–13.

Chapter Eight: A Time to Sow

1. Michael Elliott, "Paradise Lost?" *American Heritage*, February/March 1998, 62.

Chapter Nine: Cultivating the Soil

1. Diane Ravitch and Chester E. Finn, Jr., *What Do Our 17-Year-Olds Know? A Report on the First National Assessment of History and Literature* (New York: Harper & Row, 1987), 92.

2. George Barna, *Evangelism That Works* (Ventura, Calif.: Regal, 1995), 35.

3. Robert Krauss and Sam Glucksberg, "Social and Nonsocial Speech," *Scientific American* 236 (February 1977): 100–105.

Chapter Ten: Planting Part 1—The Three Tools

1. Wayne Dyer, *The Sky's the Limit* (New York: Pocket Books, 1980), 52.

2. C. S. Lewis, *The Four Loves* (New York: Harcourt, Brace, Jovanovich, 1960), 97.

Chapter Eleven: Planting Part 2—Materials

1. His four choices are *Mere Christianity* by C. S. Lewis, *The Case for Christianity* by C. S. Lewis (contained within *Mere Christianity* but also published separately), *Between Heaven and Hell* by Peter Kreeft, and *More Than a Carpenter* by Josh McDowell. Other colleagues and acquaintances have suggested additional useful titles: *Letters from a Skeptic* by Gregory Boyd,

Socrates Meets Jesus by Peter Kreeft, *The Case for Christ* by Lee Strobel, and even Eugene Peterson's creative paraphrase of the Bible itself, *The Message.* The reader may disagree with my friend's selection of "safe" books or the other titles listed above; the important point here is that we carefully consider the qualities that would make a book appropriate for the purpose of sowing.

2. James Davison Hunter, *Culture Wars: The Struggle to Define America* (San Francisco: HarperCollins, 1991), 322.

3. Woody Allen, *Crimes and Misdemeanors* (1989), available on video.

Chapter Thirteen: Sowing in the Marketplace

1. C. Bernard Ruffin, ed. *Last Words: A Dictionary of Deathbed Quotations* (Jefferson, N.C.: McFarland & Co., 1995).

2. Doug Sherman and William Hendricks, *Your Work Matters to God* (Colorado Springs: NavPress, 1987), 132.

Chapter Fourteen: Sowing to the Culture

1. Henry Blackaby and Claude King, *Experiencing God: How to Live the Full Adventure of Knowing and Doing the Will of God* (Nashville, Tenn.: Broadman & Holman, 1994), 35.

2. Ibid., 19.

3. Francis Schaeffer, *The God Who Is There* (Chicago: InterVarsity, 1968), 15–16.

Chapter Fifteen: Good Questions Answered

1. R. C. Sproul, "Right Now Counts Forever: The Christian in the Marketplace," *Tabletalk,* date unknown.

About the Author

Tim Downs is the founder of the Communication Center,
a communication training and consulting ministry of Campus
Crusade for Christ. After studying Fine Arts at Indiana University,
Tim worked for six years as a nationally syndicated comic strip
artist. He has been a speaker at FamilyLife Marriage and Parenting
Conferences since 1985 and lives in North Carolina with his wife,
Joy, and their three children.

Moody Press, a ministry of Moody Bible Institute,
is designed for education, evangelization, and edification.
If we may assist you in knowing more about Christ
and the Christian life, please write us without obligation:
Moody Press, c/o MLM, Chicago, Illinois 60610.